GW00419422

PUB WALKS in the PEAK DISTRICT

Les Lumsdon and Martin Smith

SIGMA LEISURE, Wilmslow, England

Copyright ©, L. Lumsdon and M. Smith, 1991

All Rights Reserved. No part of this publication may be reproduced, stored in a retrieval system, or transmitted in any form or by any means - electronic, mechanical, photocopying, recording, or otherwise - without prior written permission from the publisher.

First published in 1991 by Sigma Leisure – an imprint of Sigma Press, 1 South Oak Lane, Wilmslow, Cheshire SK9 6AR, England.

Reprinted 1992, 1993

Revised and reprinted 1994

Whilst every effort has been made to ensure that the information given in this book is correct, neither the publisher nor the author accept any responsibility for any inaccuracy.

British Library Cataloguing in Publication Data
A CIP record for this book is available from the British Library.

ISBN: 1-85058-246-7

Maps by
Pam Upchurch

Typesetting and design by
Sigma Hi-Tech Services Ltd, Wilmslow

Printed by: Manchester Free Press

BOOTS, BEER AND BUSES!

The Peak District is well-walked and given the outstanding beauty of the landscape, its history and culture, is it hardly surprising? The network of paths are, for the most part, in good order and this is a great bonus for ramblers who are used to finding their local paths in less desirable conditions. In contrast, the Peak District seems something of a paradise. It will only remain this way if we collectively seek to protect it by supporting the conservation work of local landowners, voluntary groups, the Peak National Park and Derbyshire County Council. They contend with over twenty million visitors every year and this cannot be an easy task. Being considerate is important.

One of the bonuses of enjoying any walk is to adjourn to a local hostelry for a good pint of ale (or other beverages) or to take respite part way around the route. Inns have for centuries welcomed customers on foot – tradespeople, farmers and farm hands going to market and, in this century, lovers of the countryside seeking their leisure pursuits at the weekend. May the tradition of hospitality and good beer remain. For the latter, we must pay tribute to the excellent work of the consumer ginger group, The Campaign for Real Ale (CAMRA). This organisation has done more for the discerning drinker than is often admitted.

There is one snag, of course, for the real ale rambler: ***Beer and driving do not mix.*** Many of the rambles in this book feature at least one pub, so those who like a drop or two should let someone else do the driving – or do as the authors did when researching the text – use the local bus! It also helps to reduce car congestion.

The walks in this volume feature the Peak District's middle ground, the limestone country known as The White Peak. There is also a companion volume for the Dark Peak.

Happy Rambling!

Les Lumsdon and Martin Smith

CONTENTS

Locations of Walks
(numbered dots correspond to the preceding contents pages)

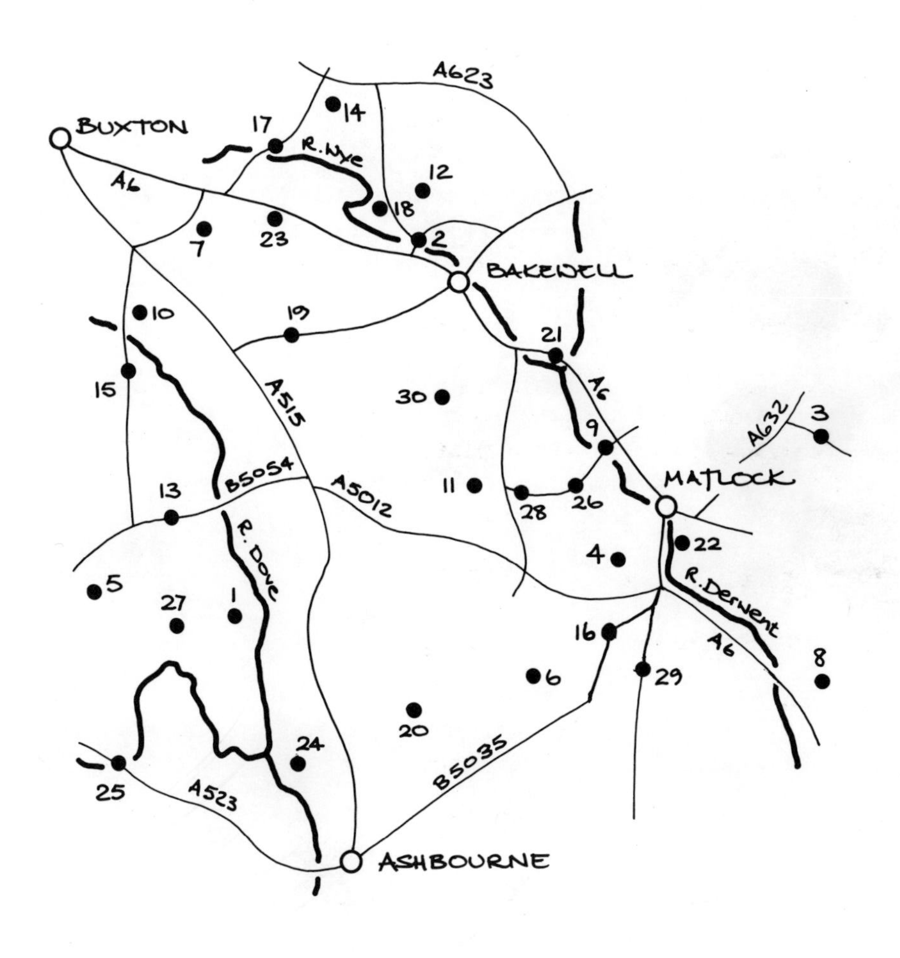

AN INTRODUCTION TO THE PEAK DISTRICT AND ITS PUBS

The exact boundaries of The Peak District are the subject of some dispute. Certainly, the towns of Buxton and Matlock would regard themselves as being within it, having for at least two centuries used their Peak District associations to attract visitors and with good effect. The boundaries of the Peak District National Park, however, are more tightly drawn, leaving out the latter two places and much fine countryside which could well have been described as being in a National Park, such as areas around Wirksworth and Matlock Bath.

This book treats such boundaries in a more liberal fashion by including walks in Crich and Ashover, for example. Perhaps it is better simply to define the Peak District more loosely as an area of moorland, dale and countryside between the major conurbations of Manchester, Sheffield, The Potteries and Derby. This is how the visitor tends to see it. Also, we have to recognise that for many it is home, the place where they live and work, a hard existence farming the hills in some cases. Most of all, it is an ancient land as rich in human culture as in the patterns of landscape, a land to be enjoyed and respected, to be husbanded and conserved for future generations. What better way to discover this place than on foot?

THE PEAK DISTRICT

The Peak District is probably more full of the presence of its past than any other region in England, for its past has not been buried in a welter of rebuilding. The isolated, rugged landscape and harshness of the climate have served to retain ample evidence of the earliest inhabitants and their successors in a way that is remarkable.

Why is this landscape, which is devoid of peaked hills, named The Peak? The truth seems to be that the earliest name was *Peac-land* meaning the country where the *Pecsaetan* people had settled. The origins of this tribe are obscure, opinion being divided on whether they were of pre-Roman or post Roman origin. Equally, their boundaries are uncertain although southwards their influence probably ceased somewhere between Crich and Belper, eastwards where the gritstone moors meet the Yorkshire, Nottinghamshire and Derbyshire coalfields, westwards where the tumbling slopes of Shining Tor meet the Cheshire plain.

Ancient Sites

Although there is now strong evidence of early settlement on the high gritstone moors, it seems likely that our original Peac-landers must have concentrated on the southern part of their territory, that part on the limestone rocks. There are many remains of early man in the limestone part of the Peak, fortresses, burial sites, dwellings and great ceremonial sites such as Arbor Low. Our earliest known trackways date from this pre-Roman time, linking these centres of population and culture together. Many survive today and are included in these walks.

The Roman occupation seems also to have concentrated on the limestone part of the Peak, where they worked and smelted lead, built their homes and bath houses, their forts and highways. The immediate post-Roman period in the Peak is almost completely a mystery but it is a fallacy to suppose that the Saxons charged in as the last legionaries marched out. There might well have been two hundred years or so before the final imposition of Saxon rule.

The Romano-British culture, therefore, survived long into the Saxon period, evidenced by place and river names such as Eccles and Derwent. Later conquerors like the Danes and Normans laid a veneer on the ancient bones of the Peakland, adding their castles and settlements but retaining the sprawling Christian parishes like Hope.

Lost Villages

Huge tracts of the Peak became royal hunting forests subjected to harsh forest law. The village of Peak Forest is a reminder of these, as is Peveril Castle at Castleton. In the Middle Ages, sometimes known as The Age of Faith, mining and agricultural development flourished in many parts of the limestone Peakland and, in others, villages vanished entirely. There are several 'lost villages', victims of The Plague or of changing patterns in land ownership and economics.

With the onset of the agrarian and industrial revolutions the scene changed dramatically again with enclosure of the open moorlands, construction of water powered mills, widening and straightening of roads. Most of the present main road network dates from the latter half of the eighteenth century and the early part of the nineteenth, leaving many of the older routes far less busy. Canals made no impact on the Peakland proper, but their railway successors left an indelible mark with their cuttings and embankments, viaducts and tunnels. Many are now gone, lamented by a population which grew up with railway travel, but many of the trackbeds remain as walking and cycling routes.

Green and Gold

The Peakland is the start of the Pennine chain known as the 'backbone of England'. At its southern end, the area covered by this book, the backbone begins to rise from the Midland plain. Its hills are threaded with walls, its fields offering shades of green and gold, hilltops often crowned with trees. The plateau land of the Limestone Peak is dissected by many deep and narrow valleys, well hidden from the surrounding hills and of very different character.

The southernmost part of the Peak is chiefly in Derbyshire but it does encompass parts of Staffordshire, particularly the Staffordshire Moorlands. The hills are not high and to confuse matters are often called 'low'. This is a corruption of the Norse 'hlaw' meaning hill and not as is usually thought, an example of Derbyshire understatement! They lack the stark grandeur of Scotland or the Lakes but the broad sweeping moorlands are appealing to the eyes nevertheless.

This southern part of the Peak has its drama, though. Along its eastern flank march the dramatic array of gritstone edges, unique in Britain. The view eastwards along the Hope Valley to Surprize, when the edges catch the rays of the setting sun, is a magnificent sight.

The gritstone edges and outcrops are the playground of the rock climber and latterly the precipitous limestone cliffs in Stoney Middleton and Matlock have become increasingly popular. The limestone landscape has its appeal too. The view of the reef hills of the Upper Dove from Crowdecote is a perpetual delight, while the rock pinnacles in Dove Dale and the towering cliffs of High Tor draw a sharp intake of breath.

Subterranean Blues

Not that all of the Peak District's beauties lie on the surface – for the limestone is riddled with subterranean passages and caves, some natural and others extended by man in search of minerals such as the famous 'Blue John' stone. Many of these caverns can be visited in perfect safety in the show caves of Matlock Bath and Castleton. The work of the lead miner and the quarry worker is explained to good effect at the Peak District Mining Museum at Matlock Bath and The National Stone Centre in Wirksworth.

However, it is probably in the valleys that the southern part of the Peak is at its best. Some wind for miles, tree clad, narrow and secretive. Most are dry but some are carved to this day by rivers, which have charmed poets and writers through the centuries, with waterfalls whose very sound is music. Several of the walks in this book venture into these dales – Matlock Gorge, the elusive Manifold, Deepdale and Cressbrookdale. They are also rich in wildlife and flowers such as the meadow cranesbill and vetches in the hedgerows.

The area covered by this book is mainly the limestone part of the Peak District known as The White Peak, so the walks are in the southern part of the Peak. The aim is to produce a companion to this issue featuring the Dark Peak and more northerly areas. The White Peak, however, is an area of both natural and industrial interest, particularly the remains of lead mining. In fact, many of the public rights of way mentioned in the text owe their existence to the mining industry as routes to work or for transporting the extracted material to other parts. Be careful not to stray from paths in these areas for while many old mines have been 'capped' by Derbyshire County Council, others have not and they are dangerous.

Lead Mining

If the story of lead mining is fascinating, so too is the story of lead itself. The tale begins some 330 million years ago when much of the southern part of the Peak was a shallow tropical sea with coral reefs and multitudes of shellfish. These shells formed the limestone. There were volcanoes in the area and, periodically, outbursts of lava covered the ocean floors and killed the corals and shellfish. These lava flows can still be discerned in places. The Bonsall walk passes a good example at Masson.

The limestones were folded and cracked over millions of years and the resultant gaps were infilled by the various minerals associated with lead: fluorspar, calcite and barytes. The mineral filled faults and cracks in the limestone may run for many miles and are known as rakes or, in a smaller version, scrins. Where the limestone was sandwiched between lava flows, the mineral takes the form of 'flats' – rather like a coal seam but usually much thinner and rarely very extensive. Where the mineral filled caverns, the result was known as pipe. Masson is the best example and can be readily visited. The minerals were formed about 180 million years ago, carried in by hot volcanic fluids which, as they cooled, deposited the various minerals in the cracks and caverns. Well over a hundred different minerals have been recorded in the Peak District ore field, some of considerable rarity.

It seems likely that lead mining was going on in the Peak before the Roman occupation. But the Romans carried the industry to new heights (depths?). They mined and smelted the lead extensively in the Matlock and Bradwell areas and transported the lead ingots, known as 'pigs', to the River Trent for shipment.

A whole body of law was laid down about this time by which the mining industry was governed. This survived through the Dark Ages to become the lead mining law in Saxon and Norman England, finally receiving written status in the *Quo Warranto* of 1287. The law was finally enshrined in Acts of Parliament in the early 1850s and still forms the basis for mineral mining in the Peak today.

Routes

Finally, to those historical features without which this book would be impossible. The footpath and road network are taken very much for granted, as are public houses on such routes. We think little of the origins of such features. Before this century the only people to travel for leisure were the rich. Walking any distance for pleasure was not fashionable. The local road and footpath network was developed essentially for workers: the route from farm and village to town, the path from cottage to farm or mine and the road from market to market.

Successive transport improvements and changes in the way in which we work have enhanced the status of some routes beyond all recognition from highway to motorway. Others have been made redundant except for pleasure, the highways of the past are now our by-ways. Many of the walks discover these ancient routes.

Peakland Customs

The Peak District is well known for its customs, from the Castleton garlanding ceremony to the procession to the chapel in Padley Gorge. By far the most pictorial is the dressing of wells in villages. Each participating village painstakingly prepares a picture made of natural materials such as flowers, twigs and leaves on a clay base. The result is one or more dressings which are placed on or near a village well as a thanksgiving for pure water. Several villages have well dressing weeks where there are shows, events or carnivals which bring communities together and delight the visitor. Tissington, mentioned in the Thorpe walk, is perhaps the best known, but look for other villages' celebrations, for they are all worth visiting.

THE WALKS

There are thirty walks of varying lengths from 3 miles to 10 miles. All of the walks include at least one public house, of course. Rather than start from the hostelry many of the routes include the pub on route. Some walks are a veritable drinker's paradise with pubs up and down dale. In these cases and indeed any instance where you are intending to quaff ale, do the travelling to and from the walk by bus, train or get someone else to do the driving. Instructions on how to reach the starting point of each walk by public transport are provided. Despite a general cut back of services in rural areas in recent years, Derbyshire is still well served thanks to the progressive attitude of the County Council and the recreational buses provided on behalf of the Peak National Park. Thus, as far as the Peak District is concerned, buses are still a relatively plentiful species. We strongly recommend you to try them!

Public Transport information can be obtained by 'phoning Derbyshire BUSLINE on:

(0332) 292200 for the Derby area

(0298) 23098 for the Buxton area

(0246) 250450 for the Chesterfield area.

Don't forget to be prepared when in the countryside for a change in weather. A knapsack with a cagoule, a snack and first aid kit is very light to carry and yet could prove to be important. Stout footwear is even more important, for some walks can get muddy. Boots are preferable although many walkers use trainers during the dry summer months.

While every effort has been made to describe these walks accurately circumstances and paths sometimes change. Stiles are particularly susceptible to damage and alteration. Stiles come in all sorts of shapes and sizes: step, ladder, squeezer or gap, the latter two mentioned being used interchangeably in this text. Treat them all with respect even though some are awkward to climb.

THE PUBS

Pubs, like humans, come in all shapes and sizes as well as having distinctly different dispositions. Virtually all the pubs mentioned in this book have one thing in common. They sell at least one real ale. For those unsure about the meaning of real ale consider the following definition quoted from 'Derbyshire Ale', The Campaign For Real Ale's guide to Derbyshire:

'The term real ale was coined by CAMRA to describe traditional British top-fermented ales brewed in the time-honoured manner with traditional ingredients – malted barley, hops and yeast – kept at the pub in vented casks which allow it to continue working, and delivered to the glass by any method that does not involve applied gas pressure.'

The proof of the pudding is in the taste. A pint of well kept real ale tastes very different from a similar brew which has been chilled and pasteurised then subjected to carbon dioxide pressure when in a keg. Choice is important too and CAMRA have been fighting over the years to ensure that the drinker has a reasonable choice of brews. If you would like to know more about CAMRA contact them at 34 Alma Road, St Albans, Herts, AL1 3BW.

Not that a pub is simply about good beer, for some prefer wine, cider or soft drinks. Rural pubs usually depend on providing food as much as drink. In some instances the food side of the business dominates and a pub becomes more of a restaurant than a place of refreshment only. One thing is for certain, without the move to providing food, many country pubs would no longer exist. The customer base of the old wayside bars has disappeared as the numbers engaged in agriculture and quarrying have declined. Many pubs have knocked down the walls between the bar and lounge to serve all comers in one larger area. Several of the pubs in this book, fortunately, still retain separate bars and have developed their outside drinking areas.

Golden Rules

There are a few golden rules to note. As pubs do consider their food trade as important they do not like ramblers eating their own food on the premises. Second, while walkers are very welcome, it is polite to remove boots – especially when muddy. This is a time honoured practice in most pubs now as there are so few traditional stone flagged bars left. So, off with the boots and make sure there are no holes in your socks!

Dogs usually have to be left outside to comply with hygiene rules, but children (well behaved ones) are almost always welcome at lunchtimes and early evenings. Sometimes, a pub is able to set aside a family room away from the bar, but please check with the landlord or landlady before settling into a particular spot, as children and pubs are governed by law.

Opening Times

Opening times for pubs still vary considerably. As a rule, most pubs mentioned in this text are open between 11 am and 3 pm, then from

7 pm in the evening. Exceptions are mentioned when we have been supplied with details by the publican. Virtually all serve food from light snacks to more substantial meals and these are usually provided six or seven days a week. At lunch times, hot food is invariably on offer until about 2 pm but at some hostelries they will serve you for the best part of a lunchtime session and from 7 pm until about 10 pm.

Beers

The beers we list are traditional cask conditioned beers on offer at the establishment mentioned. This information was correct at the time of going to print, as they say in all the best guides. The beers might vary from those mentioned, especially in the free houses listed. The range of beers is not as wide as we would wish but there are exciting brews to be found in the most unlikely places such as Timothy Taylor's Landlord in The Packhorse, Crowdecote. For those who wish to major in this subject it is essential to obtain a copy of Derbyshire Ale, The CAMRA guide to Derbyshire as soon as possible. Not only is it packed with ideas for further rambles, of the liquid variety, but it also a good read.

In Search of The Black Dog

If anyone tells you about an elusive rural pub called the Black Dog at Gratton don't be fooled. It is true that there was a sign outside a property there proudly displaying a large Black Dog and it appeared in film and television. Unfortunately, it was like most things on the television, unreal. The Black Dog happened to be a temporary set for the making of a film based on D.H. Lawrence's 'The Virgin and The Gypsy'. Ever since, people have been seeking out the Black Dog.

Enjoy the good food and refreshment at these Derbyshire hostelries but don't forget the rambles. They are a good way to burn off those extra calories. Have fun!

WALK 1: ALSTONEFIELD

Route: Hope Dale, Watts Russell pub, Wetton, Windledale Hollow

Distance: 5 miles

Start: Alstonefield village car park and toilets. Map Reference: 137551

Map: Ordnance Survey Outdoor Leisure Map No 24 – The Peak District, White Peak Area

How to get there:

By Bus – There is a limited bus service from Ashbourne and Buxton, including Sundays.

By Car – Alstonefield is signed from Hulme End on the B5054 from Hartington or from the main A515 Ashbourne to Buxton road. There is a small car park and toilet block in the village.

The George, standing alongside Alstonefield village green is justifiably popular with walkers visiting this part of the Staffordshire Moorlands in the Peak District. On many a winter's day rows of boots or cagoules can be seen lined up in the outer porch with ramblers inside warming their spirits mid way through or after a local walk. The pub has two main rooms, one on the left where children are welcome and also where food is usually served, and another on the right which tends to be cosier.

There is a campsite at the back of the pub which is available for families and this is well used throughout the season. The George sells Ansells draught beers including the premium Ind Coope Burton Ale. If you are seeking refreshment part way along the route call in at The Watts Russell Arms in Hopedale. See the route description below.

Alstonefield is one of the loveliest villages in the Staffordshire Moorlands area and is becoming increasingly popular with visitors. The church is of great antiquity but has been much restored throughout the centuries. Two scholars and friends of note, Charles Cotton and Izaak Walton worshipped here and there is a pew and pulpit belonging to

Cotton still to be seen. Near to the church is Alstonefield Hall dating from the late sixteenth century and a splendid Georgian rectory, all of which you pass at the start of the walk.

The Walk

From The George, go along the lane towards Alstonefield church. Before reaching it, however, look for a walled path on your right leading off to the right of a cottage. This path leads to a gap stile, then goes ahead to cross a stile and to exit onto a track. Go left and avoid the track turning right. Instead, keep ahead down the field and following the dry stone wall as it curves right and to a stile by a gate. Cross this and follow the path down a steep slope into Hopedale. Exit onto the road by way of a gap stile and go right. Follow this road up, past a beautiful country cottage, to the Watts Russell Arms.

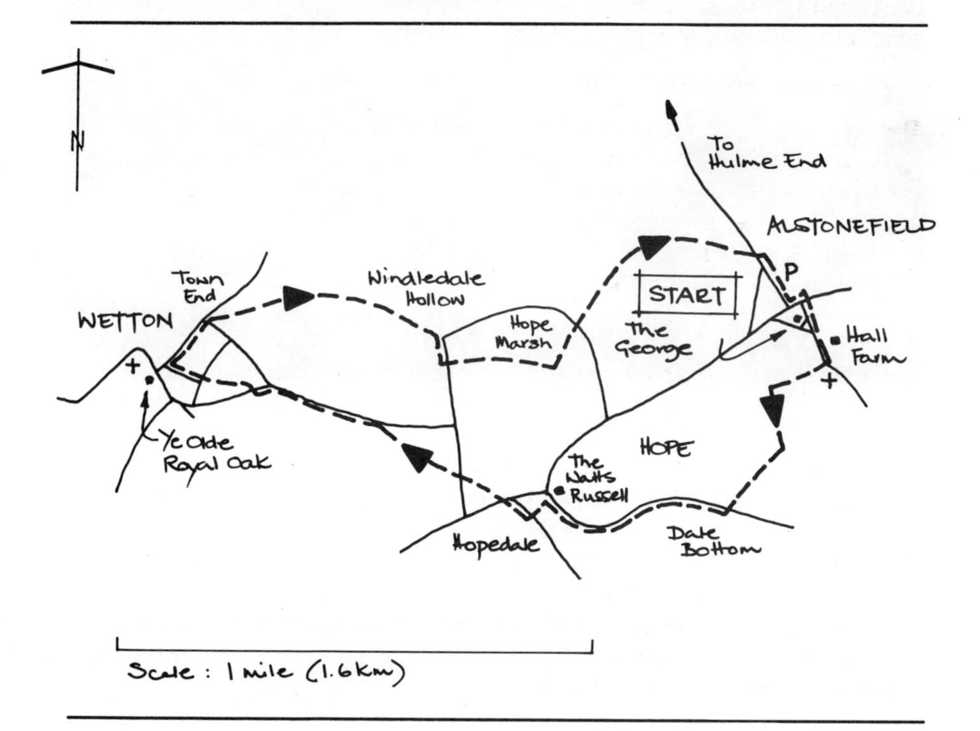

The Watts Russell

The Watts Russell pub, the unusual name reflecting the interest of a landowning family in earlier times, has two beer gardens, which are ideal in the summer months to rest awhile. It is open at lunchtimes from 1200 to 2.30 pm and 7 pm onwards during the evening serving a fine pint of Marstons Pedigree on draught and bar food up until 2 pm and until 8.45 pm in the evening.

The Watts Russell Arms

Opposite the pub, go left up a little link footpath to another road. Turn right and at the junction, cross the road and go over the stile into a field. Head slightly left to go through a stone gap stile and to cross another shortly leading onto a lane. Cross the stile on the other side and bear slightly right to a gap stile in a drystone wall. Continue ahead in the same direction to a gap stile by an electricity pole, thus leading onto a road once again.

Wetton

Turn left to walk along the road with views over to a classic dry valley broken by a tight network of drystone walls and an isloated farmstead. There's also a glimpse of Wetton church and Wetton Hill beyond. Go straight on at the junction. Very shortly afterwards go right through a gap stile opposite the barn and through a succession of stiles heading in the direction of the church. The path drops down to a gap stile leading onto a road. Turn right and walk up between houses to the village centre which is to the left, between Ye Olde Royal Oak Inn and the church.

If not stopping in the village, go right at the junction and walk past the old school and chapel. Come to Town End farm on your left and at the junction go through a gap stile ahead between the two lanes. The next section is straightforward but the stone stiles are not easily defined in places, so keep your eyes peeled. Proceed to the far right corner where you will find a gap stile. Go through it and turn left to another gap stile. Once through, proceed gently right to another gap stile to the right of a gate. Head slightly right to a stone stile before a gateway. Go over this and bear right along a green lane which gives out onto a tarmac lane by a barn.

Turn right and, in a short distance, go through a gap stile on the left. Keep ahead and cross a footbridge, then go slightly right to cross another stile. Keep ahead in this field with the hedge to your left and at the next corner go through a gap stile on the left. This leads up to a road. Cross over and cross the stile ahead. Walk up the dry valley which eventually leads to a walled track and a road. Go right here to return to Alstonefield village.

WALK 2: ASHFORD IN THE WATER

The Route: Sheldon, Magpie Mine, Great Shacklow Wood. An inspiring walk with several climbs and one steep descent.

Distance: 8 miles

Start: The Bull's Head. Map Reference: 196697

Map: Ordnance Survey Outdoor Leisure Map No 24 – The Peak District, White Peak Area.

How to get there:

By Bus – There are daily services from Manchester to Nottingham and several local services from Bakewell all of which call at Ashford.

By Car – Ashford is signed off the A6 road. There is a small car park near the Top Pump.

The Bull's Head stands back from the village road. A white building with roses around the front entrance door and seats outside which are fine on a sunny day in this sheltered alcove. If it were not for the cars parked in this tight space, the scene would be timeless, for The Bull's Head was in earlier centuries a coaching inn.

This two roomed pub has a pleasant atmosphere. The bar on the left is the usual haunt of ramblers, a cosy room with a roaring fire in winter. The larger lounge on the other side of the bar is more geared for food which is on offer at lunchtimes until two o'clock, and in the evenings. The landlord, Rodney Clarke, serves a good pint of Robinson's Best Bitter and is used to welcoming ramblers to his pub which is open weekday lunchtimes and in the evenings from 7 pm.

Ashford looks the archetypal English village with fine stone buildings wrapped around the church and river crossing. At the other end of the village stands the post office and across the road a cricket pitch, with locals watching the Sunday afternoon match. Considering the appeal of the village, it has done well to cope with the number of visitors. There is a tea shop and a place to buy gifts, but over and above this there has not been a stampede to make the place a tourist trap. Nevertheless, hundreds stop off to visit the ancient Sheepwash Bridge, and to feed the ducks on the Wye. At one time Ashford was more industrial with a small amount of mining in the vicinity, including the production of black marble ware. This is no longer the case.

The Walk

From the entrance to the Bull's Head, turn right and walk to the corner beyond the church. Turn left to pass a round canopied seat and information board before crossing the Sheepwash Bridge, noting the pound on the far bank where sheep are held before dipping in the river. The bridge dates from the seventeenth century but there were probably many other bridges on the site beforehand.

Cross the main road and turn right to walk along the pavement. At the next junction go left on the road signed to Sheldon. Within a short distance, as this curves left, bear right to cross a stile into a field alongside the river. Avoid the temptation of the low level path ahead, but instead fork left for a few paces and then right, up the steep hillside. The path levels a little as it approaches a drystone wall corner, with a broken section tumbling back down the hillside and a more robust portion leading ahead towards a wood. Follow the latter piece which should now be on your right.

This path leads to a stile by the wood, cross the stile. In the next field, continue ahead and bear slightly left to go through a gap in the next boundary wall and onwards, slightly right, to cross the next decaying wall. Proceed slightly right again towards the wood and as the valley narrows towards Sheldon, pass a mini sewerage works below to your right. The path exits at a gap stile near to a cottage in Sheldon village.

The Devonshire Arms

The thirsty walker will be disappointed here, for Sheldon no longer has a pub. It once had two but the last of these, The Devonshire Arms,

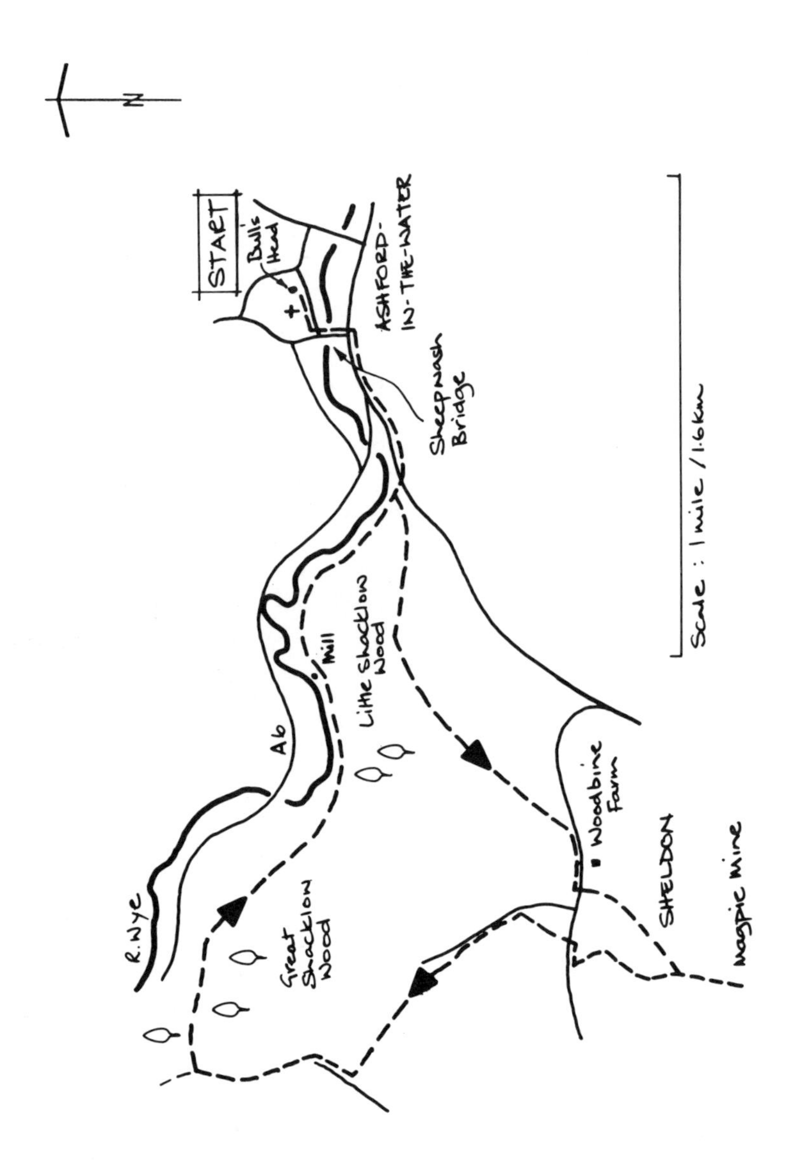
N
START
Bulls Head
ASHFORD-IN-THE-WATER
Sheepwash Bridge
Scale : 1 mile / 1.6km
Little Shacklow Wood
Mill
A6
R. Wye
Great Shacklow Wood
Woodbine Farm
SHELDON
Magpie Mine

closed many years ago. It only used to sell Ind Coope mild, drawn from the barrel in pot jugs and you could order by the quart! A tragic loss.

Turn right on the road and walk a short distance before going left through a gap stile and ahead by a barn with a drystone wall to your right. This is a short diversion to Magpie Mine, its forlorn shape now seen on the skyline before you. Cross another stile and walk through a narrow enclosure to cross a further stile. Then walk slightly left across the next small field to go through a stone gap stile and ahead again to squeeze through a gap stile on the left. Continue across the field to the mine.

Magpie Mine

The Magpie Lead Mine buildings have been preserved here including the engine house and head gear. These mines were difficult to work, accidents frequent, murder not unknown, and for little return for the miner. No wonder this place is thought to be the haunt of disgruntled ghosts. The mine was last worked in the 1950s but without success. Access is restricted but a good view can be had from the footpath at the perimeter of the mine. Retrace your steps across the field towards Sheldon and go through the stile from whence you came.

This time, however, go slightly right across the next field to cross a gap stile to join a wide green track. Go right along it to a field and then turn left through a gap stile. Head slightly left to another gap stile and ahead to another behind the buildings. This brings you to the road running through the old mining village of Sheldon, a more peaceful setting nowadays than a hundred years back.

Turn right and walk down the road for a very short distance, looking for a stile on the left just beyond the last of the cottages to your left. Cross the stile and walk through the field keeping company with the wall on the left, Sheldon chapel being on the right. Cross two stiles to drop down into a track. Turn left and leave the village behind.

The lane feeds into the fields and as it descends and curves right look for a stile on the left. Go through it and another on your right to enter a larger field. Keep ahead with a little distance between you and the drystone wall on the left. Cross a stile(with yellow marker) and three others in succession, as the path passes through a series of small fields. The final stile in this section, by a tree, leads into a lane by old mine workings. At the corner, however, leave the lane again by turning right into a field. Go through a gateway and in the next field look for a stile on the left. Cross it and walk ahead to the field corner before turning right.

At the edge of the wood, cross another stile to begin a steep descent by a fence. This section can be tricky so take it with care. Part way down the hillside the path meets a main cross path. Turn right here and walk along a narrow but delightful woodland path. It begins to drop gently at first, then more steeply as it moves closer to the perimeter fence of the river pasture. The path levels as it passes the outfall of Magpie Sough, the drainage outlet from the mine and then approaches a partly restored water mill. A lead smelter originally stood on this site, but latterly the mill was used for grinding corn. The smallest of the three water wheels powered a pump which supplied Sheldon with water.

Pass by the mill and the walk ahead through a gateway and along a track which winds its way to a step stile by another gate. Keep left to walk alongside the river bank and the last stretch to reach the Sheldon road where you began the ramble. Go over the stile and turn left to retrace your steps into Ashford.

WALK 3: ASHOVER

The Route: Ashover, Fallgate, Gregory Mine, Overton, Goss Hall, The Butts

Distance: 4 miles

Start: Ashover Village Car Park. Map Reference: 351633

Map Pathfinder sheet 761 Chesterfield

How to get there:

By Bus – There are buses to Ashover from Matlock and Clay Cross on Monday to Saturday. A daily service runs from Matlock and Chesterfield to Kelstedge.

By Car – Take the A632 from Chesterfield or Matlock to Kelstedge then the B6036 to Ashover. The car park is signed from the village centre.

The Miners Arms at Milltown is a homely public house which is open at lunchtimes between 1145 and 3 pm and with a 7pm opening during the evening. Publicans Andrew and Yvonne Guest offer really tasty food except on Monday lunchtimes when the kitchen is shut. The beers on offer at this stone built hostelry are Mansfield Riding and Old Bailey and there are seats outside when the weather is fine.

For those holding back until the end of the walk there are three other pubs in Ashover: The Red Lion serving Mansfield, The Black Swan serving Bass and The Crispin, offering Home Ales mentioned below.

Ashover has been described as a microcosm of Derbyshire. The village is situated on limestone and is surrounded by shales and gritstone, a Peak District in miniature. It is one of the largest parishes in Derbyshire and within its boundaries at one time could be found coal and lead mines, foundries, mills and a wide diversity of agricultural practice from moorland sheep farming to lowland arable farming. Now, most of the industry has gone but the village and the valley remain as delightful examples of a Peak District existence, surprisingly sundered from the rest of the area. There is a maze of footpaths and a wealth of hostelries.

The Walk

Start from the public car park by the village hall and turn left into the village. Immediately on your right is The Black Swan. Carry on towards the church with its magnificent spire and lo and behold, pub number two appears on the horizon, The Crispin. The inn sign is something special. It tells the tale of the founding of the pub after the Battle of Agincourt in 1417 and then describes an incident in 1646 during the Civil War when the landlord was expelled by drunken Roundhead soldiers.

Immediately opposite The Crispin is the Institute, built in 1860 and with an inscription in stone above the door in Latin. Go left here along a path beside the Institute and into a narrow lane with a wall on the left and hedge to the right. This runs along the back of the playing field and passes the pavilion. A gap stile gives access to a further stile leading to a lane.

There are views to the left here to the Fabrick, a gritstone outcrop perched on the rim of the Ashover valley and to Eastwood Hall, another casualty of The English Civil War. Continue along the path through a series of stiles with the wall now on your right and fields to the left, then vice versa until you emerge into a small field. Cross this to go through another stile, then follow the wall around the left hand side of the field down to a metal gate in the far corner.

Fall Hill

Go through the squeezer stile by the gate and into Fall Hill Wood. This area has been extensively worked for lead and then fluorspar, as the hillocks and hollows bear witness. On your right the trees cease abruptly and there is a cliff edge into the disused Fall Hill quarry, so keep away.

The path winds its way through the wood, emerges briefly into the edge of the field then back into the wood again before swinging left to drop

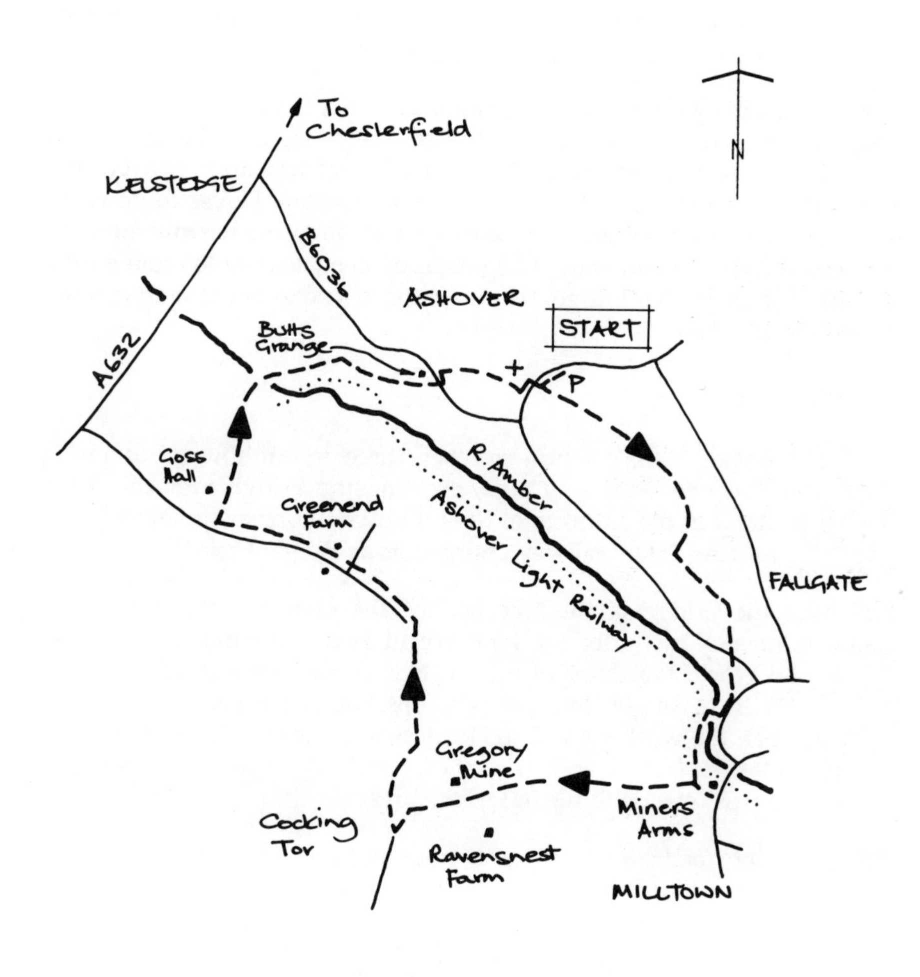
To
Chesterfield
N
KELSTEDGE
B6036
ASHOVER
A632
START
Butts
Grange
P
Goss
Hall
R. Amber
Greenend
Farm
Ashover Light Railway
FALLGATE
Gregory
Mine
Miners
Arms
Cocking
Tor
Ravensnest
Farm
MILLTOWN
Scale : 1 mile / 1.6km

down to a metal post stile. Go right here, through the gateway with the high stone wall on the left. In a short distance you emerge right on the edge of Fall Hill Quarry with its dark blue pool of water and danger signs. On the left is the derelict fluorspar plant.

Leaving this behind go through a gap stile into a field then, keeping the hedge on the right, negotiate another stile and descend the steps to a road. Take care here as the road is narrow and has no verge. Go left across the road passing Ash Meadow and Greenbank House to go right, as signed, down Greenbank House drive and along the narrow footpath between the garage and wall. It begins to descend steeply to cross a little stream by a stone slab bridge, then negotiates a squeezer stile to emerge onto a tarmac road.

Fallgate Yard

The road ahead leads to pub number three in Milltown, but pause awhile. Follow the bridleway sign, crossing the bridge over the River Amber to stand in the entrance of the Milltown fluorspar washery, better known to narrow gauge railway enthusiasts as Fallgate Yard.

Just over the bridge is the trackbed of the erstwhile Ashover Light Railway, opened just after the First World War. Although shortly after the Second World War most of the line closed, Fallgate lingered until the 1960s with increasingly decrepit waggons being shunted over muddy rails between the washery and the lorry loading ramp. The rails are still in situ under the tarmac and the station building, a ramshackle affair of corrugated iron, stands to the left of the bridge.

Return to the road and turn right, then at the next bridge follow the footpath sign, go across the river and turn immediately left. The path follows the Amber through a relatively new plantation before swinging sharply right to a junction of paths. The Miners Arms is now visible on the left so the route is decided for you. Go left, take your pick of which pair of steel posts you walk through and follow the track to the side door of the pub.

Near to the pub is a well preserved pinfold where stray cattle would have been kept for their owners to collect on payment of a fee. Grudgingly leave the pub, retrace your steps through the steel posts, at one time a level crossing of the Ashover Light Railway. Continue along the path for a short distance then at the junction turn left to recross the railway. The path climbs away from the railway by way of a short flight of steps with a wall to the left and a fence to the right. Beyond the fence are the spoil heaps of the latest mineral venture, this time for fluorspar. On the left in a clump of trees is a shaft, the remains of an eighteenth century lead mine.

Go over the chain stile and into a field, keeping close to the hedge on your right. A well defended stile in the corner of the field leads into an adjacent field and soon the path gives out onto a rough lane. Keep ahead here. The tree clad hummocky ground on the right is again evidence of old lead and fluorspar workings and, where the trees end, there is a view to Overton Hall. It was the purchase of the Overton Estate by the Clay Crows Co in 1918 that lead to the twentieth century exploitation of mineral wealth in this valley.

Continue along the lane to cross a bailey bridge which appears to span nothing but once crossed an opencast fluorspar working, now filled in. Small pools are beginning to attract plants and wildlife. There are bullrushes (Reed Mace) on the right. Keep left at the junction just beyond the bridge. Ahead now rises the bulk of Cocking Tor, a western gritstone fringe to this Derbyshire in miniature.

The lane bends left towards Ravensnest Farm then right to resume its ascent of the tor. Follow the lane past the remains of another fluorspar washery to the cottages, then go right up a path which rises sharply up the spoil banks of the fabled Gregory Mine.

Slab Fence

The main track zig zags its way up the spoil banks, passing close to the prominent chimney which is not however part of the Gregory Mine. Instead of following the track, which gets very muddy, go over to the right hand side of the spoil banks and make your way up a narrow path with an unusual stone slab fence on your right. In this particular instance it is reputed that the slabs were used from old packhorse paving but this is very unlikely as the stones show little or no signs of wear.

The slab fence becomes a wall and there is a gap. Do not go through it, however. Continue up to rejoin the zig zag path which shortly meets another track coming across the tips. Go right here and there is a fine view over Ashover Hay to Ogston Reservoir. The track leaves the spoil heaps and plunges into the wood and is wet in places. Soon a stream crosses your way from a stone trough on the left.

The path emerges from the trees and there is a fine stretch of raised stone causeway indicating that this was once a well used route. It becomes a narrow walled lane and at the crossroads you turn left along a rough lane which soon becomes a tarmac road. It joins another packhorse route coming in from the right and then swings left to skirt Greenend Farm.

The Trossachs

Continue along the lane passing Green House Farm on the left where a fine view opens up of Kelstedge village and the upper reaches of the Amber valley known locally as The Trossachs. Pass another farmhouse on the right and walk along the tree lined lane as you approach Goss Hall. Just before the hall there is a stile on the right giving out into a curious stone walled ramp and a field. Go through the stile and head down the field with the hall to the left. At the bottom of the field go through two stiles in succession, guarding an abandoned lane.

Descend across the next field with the wall to your left through another squeezer stile and to another field. To your right is the start of a little valley with an infant stream. The path passes through yet another stile then follows the course of the stream to a gateway.

The Amber

Descend now to a footbridge over the Amber. It is hard to envisage that back in 1816 there were serious proposals to canalise this river as part of a scheme to get Derbyshire lead to the River Trent at Stockwith, and hence to the navigable network. A railway was proposed instead. Even this failed to come to fruition for well over a hundred years and closed in 1951.

Once over the river cross the motorcycle course and keep going down the valley, crossing a second motorcycle track to emerge on a grassy bank. A well marked track heads off down the valley parallel to the river. A bridge is reached giving access to Butts Quarry. Embedded in the concrete of the bridge deck is a piece of railway pointwork, for this was the terminus of the Ashover Light Railway. It was the closure of Butts Quarry that lead to the demise of the line.

Carry on alongside the river, ignoring the bridge and a subsequent footbridge. Where the track swings left, follow it and then go right to a stile which requires the athletic agility of an Olympic hurdler to get over it. The journey's end is near, however, for the spire of Ashover church can be seen. Once over this stile keep left and cross a streamlet by stepping stones. Ahead is a stile, approached by a stone slab bridge, well, part of a stone slab bridge. The path twists and turns through scrub and emerges into an open field. It rises up to the left and the tip of the church spire is a landmark to look for.

At the top of the bank there is a house and a pile of stones with a gateway between. Go through it and through another gateway to emerge on a driveway which leads to the B6036. Cross over onto the footpath and go left. After a short distance, just past Butts Grange, go right through a squeezer stile, passing a barn cum garage on the left, then through another stile to the playing fields. The path follows the wall with the church ahead. A final stile takes you onto a track between the church yard and a house, beyond which a flight of steps takes you into the churchyard itself. The church is dedicated to All Saints and is a beautiful building. At the western end there is an ancient stone coffin lid. Ashover was mentioned in the Domesday Book as having a priest, church and a mill.

Leave the churchyard by a gate bringing you out by The Crispin again. Surely, the thirsty industrial archaeologist having passed so many dusty monuments is in need of a thirst quenching drink.

WALK 4: BONSALL

The Route: Bonsall, Pounder Lane, Masson Leys, Heights of Abraham, Ember Lane

Distance: 2 to 3 miles

Start: Bonsall Market Cross. Map Reference: 279583

Map: Ordnance Survey Outdoor Leisure Map No 24 – The Peak District, White Peak Area

How to get there:

By Bus – There is a bus service from Matlock on Mondays to Saturdays.

By Car – Travel on the A5012 from Cromford for one mile, then take the unclassified road signed to Bonsall from the junction near to the Pig of Lead inn. There is no public car park in Bonsall, only limited street parking, so park tidily and safely!

The Kings Head, one of Bonsall's two remaining pubs, is a two roomed local with a welcome for ramblers. The draught beer on offer is an exceedingly good pint of Tetley bitter. Bar food is also available.

Strangely, the Kings Head on the sign is that of Charles I for the date over the door is 1677 and this area was well known for its support of Parliament in the Civil War. King Charles was known to like a drop or two and many a tale is told of him straying into pubs throughout the land to greet the locals. Perhaps, that's why he seems a popular choice for pub signs to this day.

The Walk

Start from the Kings Head and walk over to Bonsall cross, a fine example of a mediaeval market stepped cross. Go up a narrow lane between the telephone kiosk and a war memorial. This is one of the

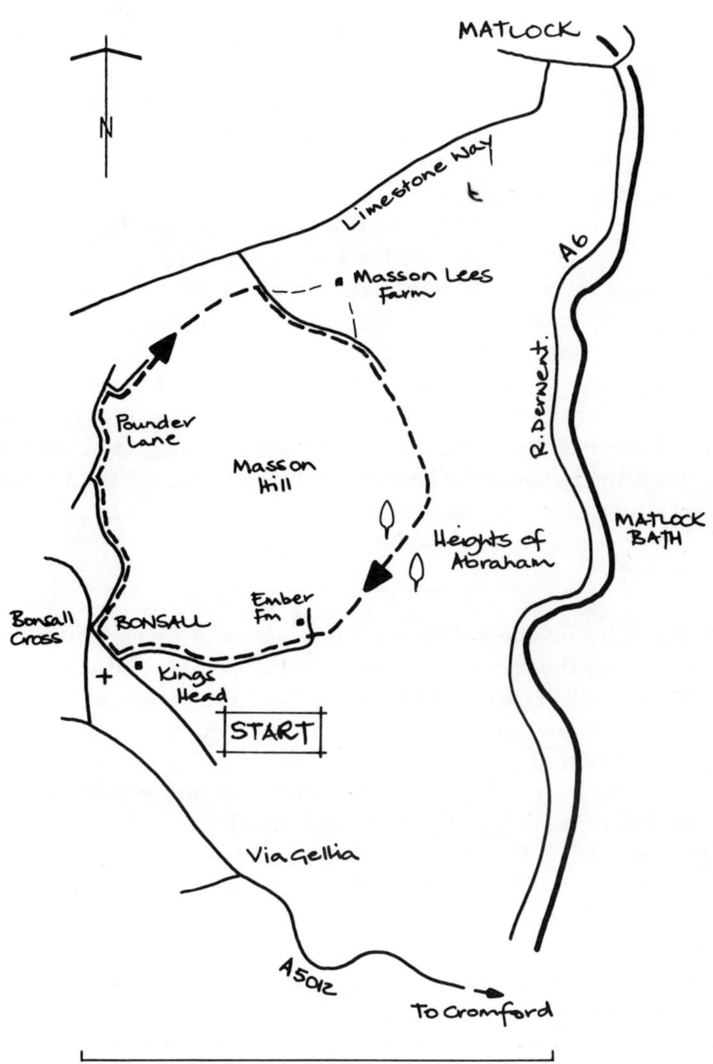
N
MATLOCK
Limestone Way
A6
Masson Lees Farm
R. Derwent
Pounder Lane
Masson Hill
MATLOCK BATH
Heights of Abraham
Ember Fm
Bonsall Cross
BONSALL
Kings Head
START
Via Gellia
A5012
To Cromford
Scale : 1 mile /1.6 km

ancient pack horse routes which converge on Bonsall and by which all lead ore was at one time carried. The first section of the lane is concreted as it was used in the 1950s by lorries for transporting the locally extracted fluorspar.

The lane climbs steeply, soon leaving Bonsall behind but with increasingly good views over the village to the small hamlets of Upper Town and Slaley. A network of narrow lanes and paths link these settlements more directly than the motor roads, and some of these walled lanes can be seen as you look across the valley. The concrete soon disappears at a gateway where the track continues up the hillside past obvious traces of mineral working. This was part of the Great Rake which outcrops extensively on the eastern side of the hill at Matlock Bath. Your way swings left and narrows between walls and hedges – it can be decidedly muddy at times. A short distance further on, there is a chance to break out of the confines of the lane where a footpath joins on the left. From this point, there are two rights of way, the lane itself and beside it, on the left, a path. Those wishing to avoid the mud should take the latter route.

Leadwort

Continue gently up the hill offering fine views of Bonsall and Via Gellia to your left and the remains of the fluorspar working to your right. Old workings are readily identified by the line of hummocks and hollows, each a separate shaft and characterised in a way with a distinctive flora and fauna such as the delicate white flowers of *Minuatiae Verna,* known locally as Leadwort. Newer workings tend to suffer from the modern phenomenon of instant restoration, with the hummocks being flattened, the opencasts back filled and the new surface given a liberal dose of 'Motorway Mixture' to secure quick grass growth. Unfortunately, the lead tolerant species which make the old lead rakes their home lose out, and recent checks on this site revealed neither Leadwort nor the other common spoil tip plant, Alpine Pennycress.

The path rejoins the lane at a stile for a final muddy slide down to the junction with another deep cut hollow way. This is Pounder Lane. Go right and resume the ascent of the hill. The hollow way widens out to a cart width, being an access point to the old workings. The parallel footpath also resumes, again on the left hand side. This soon rejoins the main lane near a gateway, but this is not too obvious. The view back over Bonsall extends to Harboro' Rocks and the Golcanda Mine (now Hopton Minerals). At this point a path carries on northward, a continuation of the pack horse route to Jug Holes and Darley Dale. Pounder Lane bears right for Salters Lane and Matlock. Your way is a third route, no more than a path, but signed, passing through a gap stile in the wall to the right and heads east, slightly left across the field to cross a narrow disused lane and then pick up a curious wide and walled lane.

Masson

This is part of an ancient route from the Mettesforde over the Derwent (near to where Matlock Bridge now stands) to Uppertown and Grangemill, Minninglow and Leek. As such it is part of the old salt routes from which the nearby Salters Lane takes its name. The path soon emerges onto a broad track once used by the Masson fluorspar working. Go across the track onto a narrow path, then over a stile to the right and follow the distinct waymarked path left and downwards into the Derwent valley. Signs here proclaim that you are on the Limestone Way and also the Masson Site of Special Scientific Interest. The latter site is the focus of immense geological interest but also features lead tolerant flora in and around the very interesting industrial archaeological remains.

Be Warned

The geological interest is centred on the fact that Masson Hill comprises a mass of limestone, trapped between two layers of volcanic lava. At the junctions of the lava and limestone there has been a chemical reaction to form the dolomite limestone. In water-formed caverns in the limestone there were rich mineral deposits of lead ore, fluorspar and barytes. The mineralisation, unusually for Derbyshire did not form very long narrow veins or rakes but here has taken the form known as 'pipes'. Hence the pock marked appearance of Masson hillside, with its innumerable old shafts. Be warned, however, that these relics are very dangerous. Do not wander – keep to the recognised footpaths.

Continue down the hill with fine views across the Derwent valley. Soon a track is reached cutting across the path. Go right here and follow the track onto Masson hillside. This is one of several in the area created as a result of the workings. The 'old man', i.e. the early lead miner had the right of access to his lead mine from the nearest public highway in a direct manner as possible. This was agreed by the Barmote, the miners' court, and the width of the access was determined by two men walking side by side with arms outstretched and fingers just touching. In reality this would just allow passage for a horse and cart.

The track skirts around the back of Masson Leys Farm before descending to join up with another track rising from the left. Continue on this track through a series of fields with grassed spoil heaps, until the path emerges onto open hillside. Ignore tracks leading off left and right, continuing steadily upwards. To the left, there is a stupendous view over Matlock to High Tor and Riber, while to the right are the gaunt remains of the winding gear of Black Ox mine, last worked in the 1950s.

Mrs Sugden's Level

A track on the left leads down to Mrs Sugden's level, another 1950s venture which failed to reach ore bearing rock was abandoned and flooded. It still has its railway and winding gear. Until recently there was a waggon at the surface, but this has been pushed into the mine and is now under water too.

The path shortly passes a picnic table above the exit of the Masson cavern, a former lead mine turned show cave. This is part of the Heights of Abraham complex and a good path leads down to the Victoria Tower, restaurant and viewpoint over Matlock Bath. If you do not intend to visit the Heights and its caverns follow the track through a gateway down to another gate then right along the waymarked path around the grounds and into the woodland overlooking Matlock Bath.

The path emerges from the woodland, fights its way through an area of scrub, dips and crosses another lead rake, again last worked in the 1950s for fluorspar. A little further, at a junction of paths, virtually a cross roads, go right and enter Ember Lane near Ember farm. The lane soon becomes a walled track with views to the south over Via Gellia and Middleton. Follow the lane as it descends gently into Bonsall. Turn right at the T junction by the church and continue down until you reach the cross where the walk began.

WALK 5: BUTTERTON

The Route: Hoo Brook, Ossoms Hill, Grindon, Hillsdale. Be prepared for a fair climb up the shoulders of Ossoms Hill to Grindon village. Otherwise, the going is relatively easy and there are many pleasant views.

Distance: 5 miles

Start: By the church at Butterton. Map Reference: 076576

Map: Ordnance Survey Outdoor Leisure Map No 24 – The Peak District, White Peak Area

How to get there:

By Bus – There is a very limited service from Leek. Contact Staffordshire Busline (0785) 223344

By Car – Butterton is signposted off the B5053 which leaves the main Leek to Ashbourne road at Bottom House. From the north the B5053 leaves the main Buxton to Ashbourne road at Brierlow Bar near Buxton. There is a little parking around the church at Butterton so please park considerately.

There are two pubs and a superb tea room and restaurant mentioned in this ramble, The Black Lion in Butterton, The Cavalier in Grindon and The Manifold Arts Centre back in Butterton. A nice idea is to prime yourselves for the walk at the Black Lion which serves Scottish and Newcastle beers including Theakstons on draught. The pub offers meals and has several bars to choose from, each one of a different character. The hosts are used to ramblers calling in and for those who have forgotten their map, there's an opportunity to take a look at the one on the wall by the toilets. There's also accommodation available here for those who fancy a few days exploring this splendid part of the Staffordshire Moorlands, one of the quietest parts of the Peak District. There are seats outside facing south so when the sun shines it is a lovely spot. The initial over the door of this old pub is thought to be that of the builder. No doubt, he supped a pint or two when the job was done.

The second establishment to mention is the Cavalier, another remarkable survivor in these isolated parts serving the high level hamlet of Grindon, the mid way point on your ramble. According to the locals the pub has only been in existence during this century. It was a farmhouse and undertakers in previous times. A press cutting on the bar wall tells the tale of how this pub declared for the side of the Royalists only thirty years or so ago!

The building dates from 1640 and has several fascinating features including oak beams and stone features. The pub is reputed to be haunted especially by the ghost of a ten year old girl. In recent times a barmaid locked herself in the kitchen after a ghostly sighting!

The publicans, Andrew and Yvonne Easom serve Sheffield best bitter on handpump and very often another guest beer. They also offer food in the lounge areas around the bar. There are seats outside with stone tables and comfortable wooden benches as well several Victorian agricultural implements on show.

The Walk

From the church, walk down the hill past the Black Lion and Manifold Arts Centre. The road curves right and then left to reach the ford. Turn left here(signposted) along an access track towards a cottage. Before reaching it, cross the brook on your right and then walk to the left along a narrow strip. Go over a stile and then through a gap out of the fold. Walk down the field with the Hoo Brook on your left. Cross the stile ahead and through a gap in the next boundary. Continue down the valley in this way until you reach stepping stones across the brook to the other side. The path is reasonably well worn and the way is signed over the stream so you should not miss it.

Ossoms Hill

Cross the stile on the other side and turn right to follow the brook once again but on the other bank. After a further short stretch you come to something of a junction. Cross the stile by the footbridge and then another on the right before crossing the bridge. This leads into an area

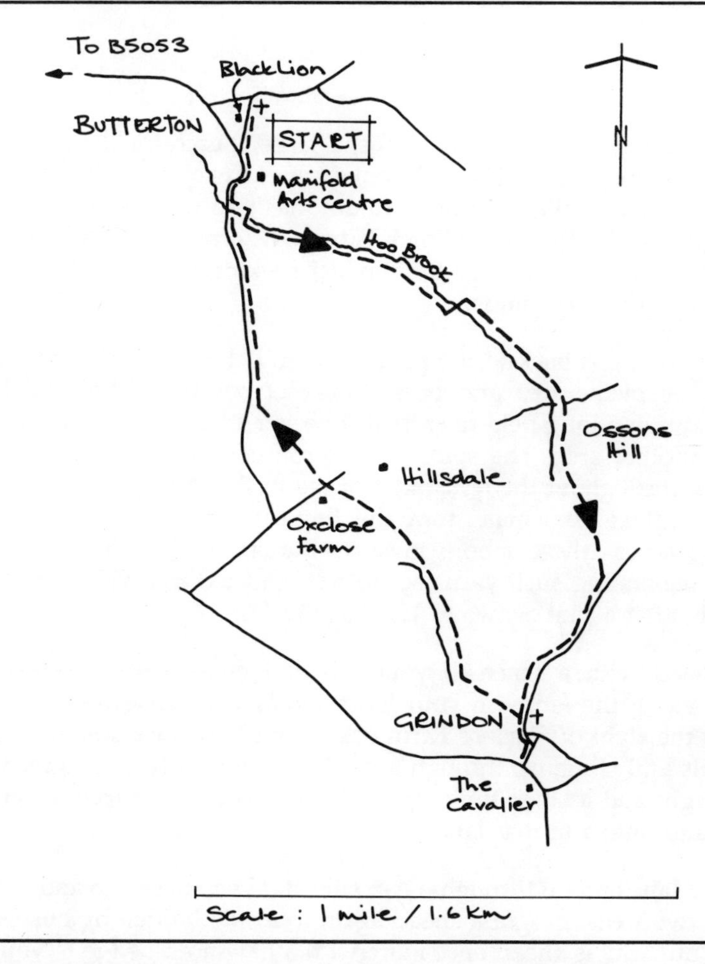

known as Ossoms Hill, a wooded edge rich in wildlife. It now belongs to The National Trust.

The path begins to climb with a tributary brook on the right at first. It then heads slightly left to cross a stile and passes a line of hawthorns just beyond. Climb the hillside and cross a stile on your right by a gate and keep ahead with a hedge on your right. Cross a stile by another gate and head across the field, slightly right, to join a lane. Turn right here to walk up to Grindon church and, just beyond, to a road junction where you turn right and then ahead at the next one. Within a matter of paces you are at The Cavalier.

Grindon

Grindon church dates from the 1850s, a large church for the size of the congregation these days, but well looked after. Its spire, like Butterton's, is a landmark for miles around. Grindon has two professionally trained village guides, the Hulmes at Porch Farm, who arrange walking holidays and offer accommodation for the rambler seeking to stay in this part of the Staffordshire Moorlands.

Retrace your steps back to the picnic site and church. Go left to cross a stile by the picnic area and pass a derelict building. The path keeps ahead through a long field to cross a squeezer stile, then through a short field to another stile. The spire of Butteron church comes into sight, a landmark throughout the remainder of the walk. One local legend has it that a headless horseman from the English Civil War is often seen galloping across these moors towards Butterton. The Victorians were good at generating such yarns so do not read too much into the story, especially after a pint or two in The Cavalier.

Keep ahead with a fence to your left and cross a stile and stream. Proceed along the fence on your left to cross a further stile. Then head towards the right of Oxclose Farm below and look for a stile in the dip. Cross this and climb up through a muddy section between a green barn on the right and a stone building to the left. The path curves around to the left and onto a tarmac lane.

Cross the lane and go through a gap stile and keep ahead to another stile beneath two trees. Progress ahead again to a stile hidden by bushes and a tree. Your way is ahead once more with a hawthorn hedge to your left. Cross another stile and go through a short field. Go through a gap stile and then go slightly right to a further gap stile. Now follow the hedge on your left, resisting the temptation to exit through a gap at the corner. Walk a little further to cross a stile which joins the lane almost opposite the barns on the other side.

Turn right on the road and walk down the hill to the ford at Butterton and then climb up the bank, following the right fork, to reach The Manifold Arts Centre possibly in time for afternoon tea.

WALK 6: CARSINGTON

The Route: Carsington, Carsington Pasture, Brassington, Harboro Rocks, Golconda, Old Knoll

Distance: 4 to 5 miles

Start: Carsington village. Map Reference: 252533

Map: Ordnance Survey Outdoor Leisure Map No 24 – The Peak District, White Peak Area

How to get there:

By Bus – There is an irregular bus service from Ashbourne, Wirksworth and Matlock on Mondays to Saturdays. A seasonal Sunday service runs from Ashbourne and Matlock.

By Car – Travel on the B5035 from Ashbourne and Cromford to the western end of Carsington by pass then turn right as signed into the village. There is a limited amount of on street car parking but please park considerately.

The Miners Arms at Carsington is a traditional village pub serving draught Bass by electric pump. The pub is full of brass ornaments and has a pleasant feel about it. In recent years it has featured in The Derbyshire real ale guide. Food is served at lunchtimes and there are seats outside.

If you are seeking a pub on the route there are two in Brassington, The Miners Arms, nearer to The High Peak Trail and the amazing Olde Gate Inne, a place not much altered over the years. The latter pub is thought to date from the early part of the seventeenth century and is a must for the rambler. It is open at lunchtimes throughout the week. Both houses serve Marston's beers.

The Walk

At the western end of Carsington village, the main road turns sharp left but the lane to Brassington goes straight ahead past several fine houses. Follow the narrow lane which after the last house, deteriorates to a cart track from which there are views south to Carsington Water. This project has been one of the most keenly fought and also most bedevilled by problems since construction began. Now it is completed it has become a major visitor attraction in the area. It is well worth a visit.

Cart Track

The cart track continues easily around the side of the hill to Carsington Pastures, at one time an area of intense mining activity. Mining finally ceased in 1919. The track passes a small quarry on the right and soon leaves the confines of wall and hill to enter Carsington Pastures proper. Somehow, possibly because of the mining, this area escaped the Enclosure Acts and is largely open. Leave the track now and head up the hill through a strange little cutting which is probably the remains of the worked-out Flaxpiece Head Rake. Emerging from the cutting the path picks its way across Perseverance or White Rake to a gap stile in a ruined wall. The path clips the corner of the next field and goes through another stile to enter the natural bowl of Wester Hollow. There are limestone outcrops on your left and right as the path heads down to a stile roughly in the middle of the wall opposite.

Pass over this stile and head towards the left hand corner of the barn where there is another stile. You now enter a lane which served as access to Wester Head Mine on your right, famous for its white lead ore. Go over the track and a stile to return to fields again. A trackway leads upwards, curving to the right as it leaves Wester Hollow.

Brassington

The tractor way terminates abruptly in an area of ruined buildings and spoil heaps of a former mine. Before reaching this point, the path leaves on the left to pick its way carefully through the hummocks and hollows of Nickalum mine. The path becomes more distinct as it descends towards Brassington. Once through a stile, go alongside a wall until, by

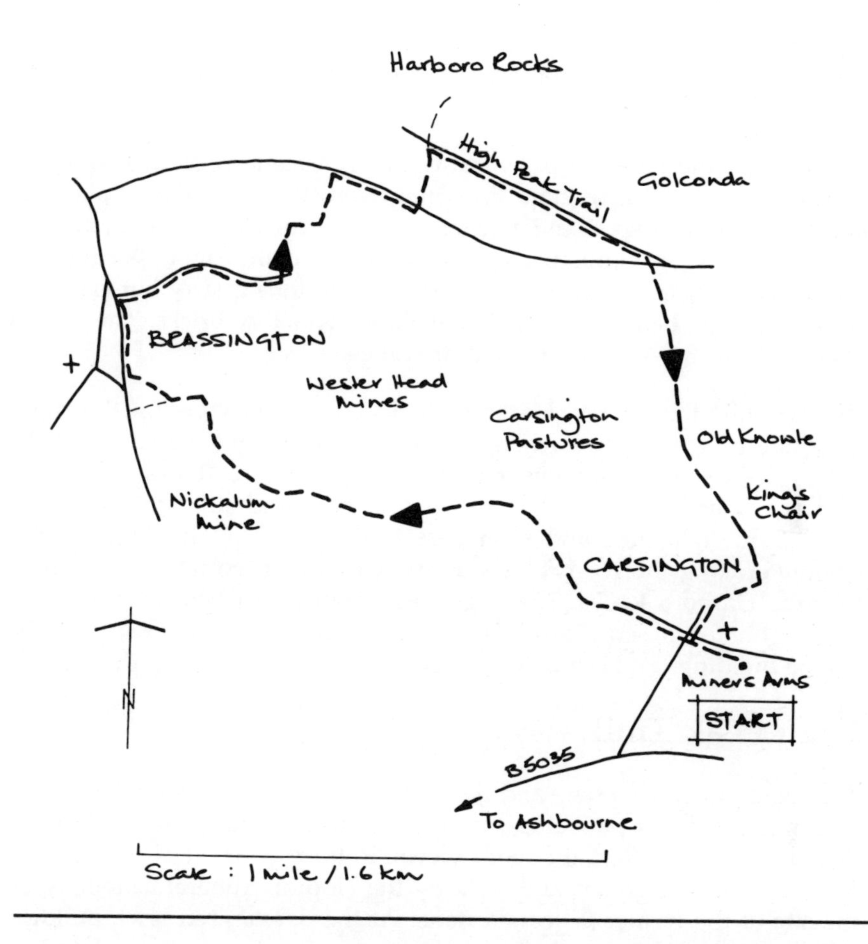

the thorn trees, there is a further stile on the left which leads into fields adjacent to the village. Seek out a stile in the wall to the right and head across the next field towards a yellow shed, previously a National Carriers lorry body. Near the shed you will spot a stile, reached by a short flight of steps. Go left here through the buildings and onto the main road in Brassington. If you are not stopping go right here.

If you are visiting the pubs, go over the road and make your way into the heart of the village. Then retrace your steps to the point where you entered the village and go past the village hall. At the road junction take the lane to the right with a 'No Through Road' sign. This was once the main route into Brassington from the east but it has been severed by quarrying.

The start of the lane is up a narrow dry limestone dale with unusual views back over Brassington. Emerging from the dale onto a plateaux again a mound of spoil and a fence block the road but a footpath goes left through a gate and then follows a fence to the right, skirting the quarry workings. Unusually, this is not a limestone quarry but clay and silica sands are being extracted for making refractory bricks. The clay is also used for the Wirksworth well dressings.

As you skirt the quarry, Harboro Rocks come into view on the right. Continue by a wall and where this turns sharp right, head across the field towards the green tower structure by Harboro Rocks. When the wall is reached again, go left, down to a gate and stile exiting onto a road. Turn right here and soon pass the entrance of the brick works. Continue along the road for about 100 yards then go left along a path towards Harboro Rocks. The High Peak Trail is reached after the path has negotiated a scrapyard. Follow the path across the trail, past the ruined buildings and out onto the open hillside at the foot of the rocks.

High Peak Trail

The rocks rise in two tiers and there are a variety of ways up, from easy to dangerous. Your path ahead is obvious on the ground and a trig point is soon reached, offering superb views. Retrace your steps to the High Peak Trail. Here, go left and walk by the Hopton Mineral Company on the site of the former Golconda mine. At the derelict red brick building follow the signposted path on the right to a road. Cross the road and go over a stile, now heading back to Carsington Pastures. The stump of an old windmill can be seen to the left.

King's Chair

The path follows the wall and telephone line over Old Knowle and then the wall kinks left and right to the curiously fashioned Kings Chair. This is an outcrop of dolomite limestone, artificially fashioned into a throne shape during the eighteenth century. Make your way back to the telephone line and follow this steeply downhill alongside the beautifully named Children's Fortune workings.

There seems to be no way out at the bottom of the hill. Do not despair. Just to the left of the house which backs onto the hillside there is a little gate with a notice saying 'Footpath down steps'. This is the case, for the path goes past an outbuilding, swings left and through the garden before widening into a lane. This leads to the main road where the walk began. The Miners Arms lies a short distance to the left along the main road.

WALK 7: CHELMORTON

The Route: Pomeroy, Pasture Barn, Town Head. Mostly easy walking.

Distance: 7 miles

Start: Chelmorton church. Map Reference: 114703

Map: Ordnance Survey Outdoor Leisure Map No 24 – The Peak District, White Peak Area

How to get there:

By Bus – There is a limited service from Buxton.

By Car – Travel on the A515 Ashbourne to Buxton road and turn onto the A5270 link road to the A6. Chelmorton is signed from the A5270.

The Duke of York at Pomeroy stands prominently alongside the main Buxton to Ashbourne road. It is thought to date from the fifteenth century. The name has also been associated with the Duke of York of this century who is reported to have been seen in the pub with Mrs Simpson. He planted the tree in front of the pub which is growing so strongly now. Despite this, the sign is of Richard, Duke of York, who became Richard III.

The Duke of York pub is situated mid way on the ramble so is an ideal stopping place. It has a spacious bar to the left and a smaller bar on the right leading to a restaurant area. There are also garden areas outside. It is often said that Robinson's beers are hard to keep but the reader will be rewarded here, for the Best Mild and Bitter have been found to be in tip-top condition by the authors when on their quality control exercises! The pub opens lunchtimes throughout the week with a 6 pm opening in the evenings. The drinking hours are standard for Sundays but this pub has a special licence allowing it to serve food all day on a Sunday. It is a good all round pub for there is a lovely balance between locals working in nearby quarries or farms and visitors using it.

The Walk

Start from the Church Inn at Chelmorton, a smaller pub with some seats outside. It serves very tasty Marstons draught beers and tends to concentrate on laying out tables for food thus leaving only a limited space for drinking around the bar. Chelmorton is one of the Peak District's quieter villages being slightly off the beaten track. The village is mediaeval in shape with one main street and little tracks leading off into thin strips of land. These have been enclosed for centuries, and are some of the finest examples of early enclosures in the country.

Walk down the entire length of the main street until it comes to a crossroads. This is the site of the mediaeval town ditch. Cross the road and turn left to walk facing the traffic. At the corner go over a stone step stile into the field and head slightly right up the hill to cross another step stile. Proceed slightly right again to cross a wooden stile followed by a stone stile and keep ahead with the drystone wall on your right to a lane. Turn right along the lane.

Pomeroy

This rough track eventually gives out onto a tarmac road but turn left immediately here over a stone step stile and keep ahead, following the drystone wall on the right. Cross a stile and continue ahead to cross another boundary wall before crossing a stile by an electric telegraph pole. Walk over to the opposite field boundary wall and turn left. Go through the gap and walk to the corner of the field where a stile exits onto the main road. Along the road to the right is an impressive boundary stone marking the different quarters of the Hartington township or parish. Turn left and walk the short distance to the Duke of York at Pomeroy.

Just beyond the pub car park you will find a stile on the left. Cross it and head slightly right to a gap stile in the wall. Walk diagonally left across this next field to cross a drystone wall approximately halfway down. In this next field, head diagonally across to the far left corner to cross two stone stiles in succession. Head for a gateway in the far wall towards a spinney of trees. Walk through the two gateways by the spinney and along the drystone wall to exit onto a lane.

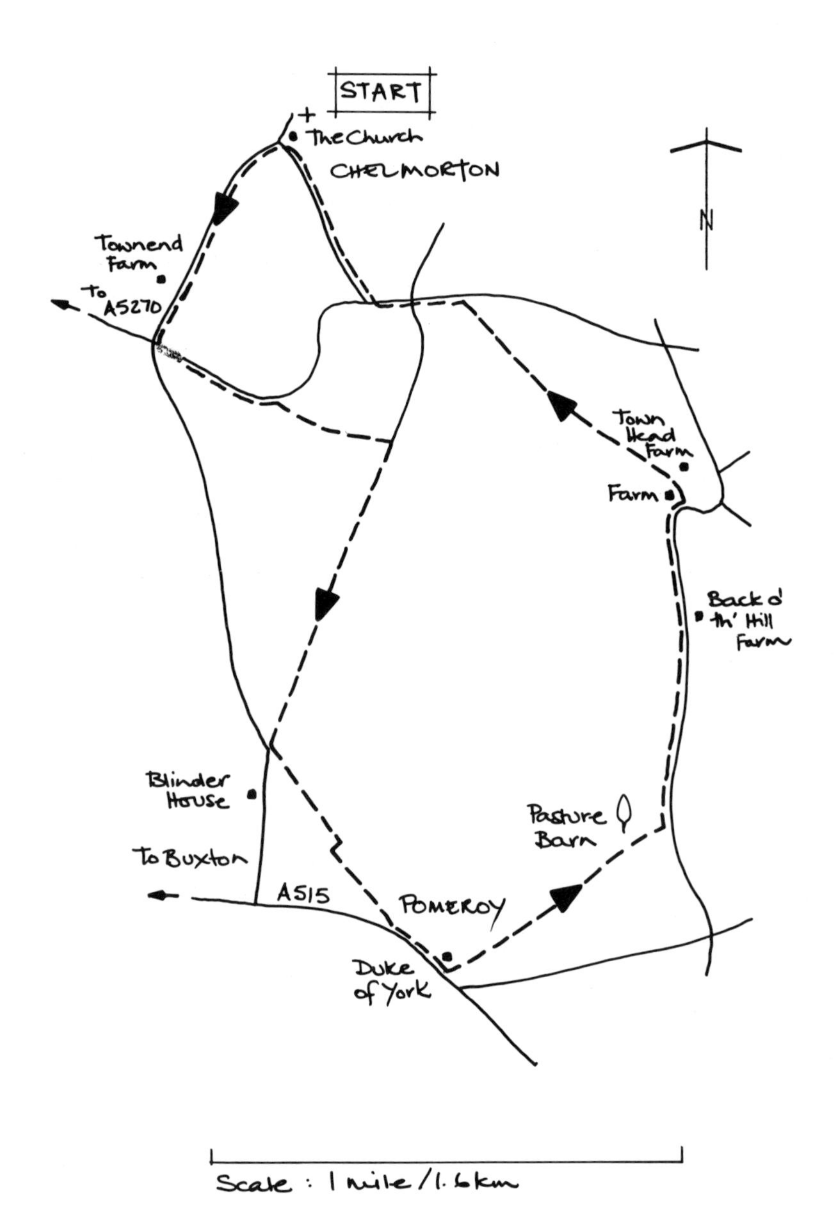
START
The Church
CHELMORTON
N
Townend Farm
To A5270
Town Head Farm
Farm
Back o' th' Hill Farm
Blinder House
Pasture Barn
To Buxton
A515
POMEROY
Duke of York
Scale : 1 mile/1.6km

Turn left and walk towards Flagg along this pleasant lane, passing Back 'O 'Th Hill Farm. Not far beyond look for a stile on the left by a farm entrance to High Stool Farm as the road veers sharp right. Your right of way is over the stile signposted in two directions. Cross another stone stile by a barred gate and swing around to the right of the mound with the walled woodland ahead. Go over the next stile by the gateway and your way is diagonally across to a mid field stone stile, then ahead to the top left corner of the next field, i.e. heading slightly left. Go over another stone stile and continue towards a tree, the stile being just to the left of it.

Fine Views

Bear slightly left away from the drystone wall climbing over the bank towards the far left corner where a tarmac road is joined. Go left but take the second turning right back to Chelmorton with fine views overlooking the village. In a short distance, there is a path signposted on your left. Go through the gap stile and drop down to a gateway leading into a concrete drive. Go down this to the main street of Chelmorton, turning right for the church.

WALK 8: CRICH

The Route: Crich Marketplace, The Tors, Chadwick Nick, Crich Chase, Bilberry Wood, Cromford Canal, Thurlowbooth, Chasecliff, Benthill, Tramway Museum

Distance: 4 to 5 miles

Start from Crich marketplace. Map Reference: 350542

Map: Ordnance Survey Outdoor Leisure Map No 24 – The Peak District, White Peak Area or Pathfinder sheet no 794 Crich and Bullbridge.

How to get there:

By Bus – There is a daily bus service from Alfreton and Matlock.

By Train: There is a daily train service between Derby and Matlock calling at Whatstandwell where there is a steep 1 to 2 mile walk to Crich. It is also possible to alight at Ambergate and walk along the A6 a short distance to a canal bridge over the Cromford Canal and join the walk there.

By Car – Travel on the A610 from Ambergate or Ripley to Bullbridge, then follow the signs to Crich. There is parking available in the marketplace.

The Cliff Inn has been in the Good Beer Guide for 13 years, so what better testimony could there be for this local pub which serves Kimberley Best Mild, Best Bitter and Classic, all of which are hand pulled. Your hosts, Beryl and Roy Calladine, are more used to tram drivers calling in rather than ramblers, but either way you can be assured of a friendly welcome.

There are two bars often buzzing with the concerned gossip of The National Tramways Museum. There is a little outside seating in the car park. The Cliff is open lunchtimes throughout the week and offers good food at lunchtimes and from 6pm during the evening.

The National Tramway Museum, almost next door, is an essential visit, for it has exhibits of varying ages from the UK and overseas. Admission includes a ride on a tram and this is most enjoyable. While the rest of Europe retained the tram and still cherishes them as a means of easing urban congestion, Britain abandoned its many systems. However, both Manchester and Sheffield now have trams back in their streets and other cities are set to follow.

The National Tramway Museum, Crich (reproduced by permission)

If time permits, you should also aim to visit Crich Stand by walking up the road past the museum and then bearing left. The first tower was built on Crich Hill (939 feet) in 1788 as a viewing platform offering fine views for miles around. In 1851, a stone tower was built but was struck by lightning in 1901. Following the First World War, the local regiment – The Sherwood Foresters – decided to use this site as a regimental war memorial and built a new tower.

The Walk

Leave the marketplace via Sandy Lane, to the right of the Baptist Chapel. Where the lane levels out, by the 30 mph signs, there is an excellent view eastwards. Here also is a narrow track on the left. Go along this for a short distance and look right to see the mouth of the old tunnel which carried George Stephenson's Crich Mineral Railway under Sandy Lane. The line was opened in 1841 to bring limestone from Crich Quarry to the limeworks at Ambergate. It closed in 1857 and the rail was lifted and taken to the Talyllyn railway in Mid-Wales for use there. Unusually, the gauge was 3 feet 3 inches or metre gauge.

Return to Sandy Lane and go left up to the Fire Station. On the left, there is a footpath sign which directs you onto a path along The Tors. This is a gritstone edge which commands enormous views to the east and, once you are into open fields, there is an equally good view to the west. The view back discloses the limestone edge of Crich Quarry with Crich Stand perched on top of it. The Tors, however, end abruptly at Chadwick Nick and the path swings left over a stile and steeply down to the road in its deep cutting. The Crich Mineral Railway used to cross this road on the level about 100 yards further along to the left.

Go right at the road, through the Nick (but be careful as there is no footway) and down the road to a sharp right hand bend. There are views over the Derwent Valley to Shining Cliff Woods and Alderwasley Hall. At this bend go left over a blue stile and onto a footpath, keeping the wall on your left. The path goes through two fields in this manner before coming to the very brink of the Derwent valley and the edge of Crich Chase. Go left here (there's not much choice) and skirt the edge of the valley, accompanied by the dull hum of traffic below.

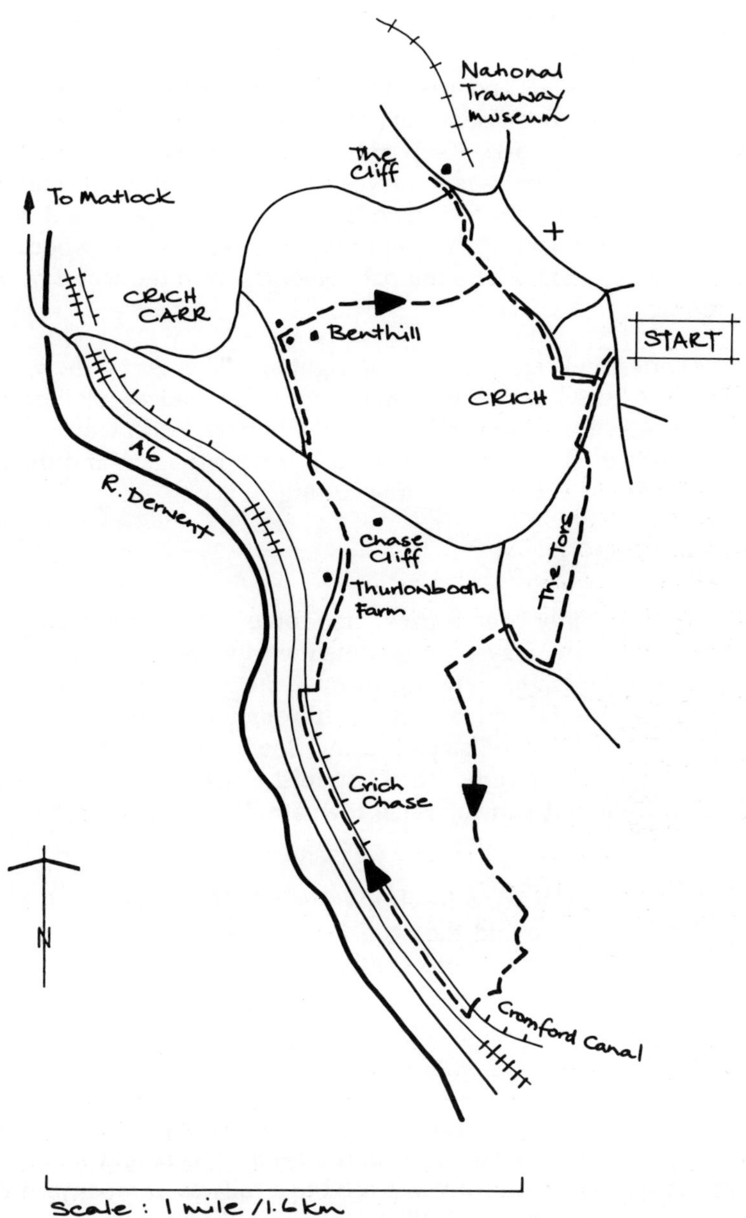
National
Tramway
museum
The Cliff
To Matlock
CRICH
CARR
Benthill
START
CRICH
A6
R. Derwent
Chase
Cliff
Thurlowbooth
Farm
The Tors
Crich
Chase
Cromford Canal
N
Scale : 1 mile / 1.6 km

Crich Chase

The path is well trodden and easy to follow as it enters the oak and birch woodland of Crich Chase, a very beautiful section of the walk. Just past a gateway, the path forks. Keep right, descending through a shallow cutting, then follow the path as it curves left and goes through another gateway. The Ordnance Survey map shows this as open land with scattered trees but the whole area might now be described as woodland except for one open field where the path emerges from the wood near a ruined building.

The path now descends steeply, curving right and re entering the wood. There are many tracks and paths interlacing this wood so vigilance is required, although the main path is clearly defined except at a point where it forks. Bear left to join another track, keep left again and then at once fork right down a narrow shallow cutting.

Packhorse Route

This has almost certainly been a packhorse route at some time and, like so many of these hollow ways, can become muddy after wet weather. At the gate and stile go right, now in an open field, heading diagonally across to a gate in a far left corner. Go through the gate, noting the spring on the left with stone steps leading down to it. At the track go right and over the bridge across the Cromford Canal. Immediately over the bridge, go right and join the canal towpath. Walkers using the train to Ambergate can join the route at this point.

Just on the Cromford side of the bridge is a half sunken work boat, pointed at both ends to avoid the need for turning. It is a crudely built vessel but not beyond restoration. A little further on are the remains of an old wharf.

Cromford Canal

The next mile or so along the canal banks is easy going. The Cromford Canal was opened in 1793, the main traffic being in coal and limestone. Like many canals the Cromford was leased to a railway company, in this instance the Midland Railway in 1852. It was finally purchased outright in 1870. By 1899 traffic at the Cromford end was down to 3 to 4000 tons of coal upwards and less than a 1000 tons of stone downwards. A collapse in Butterley Tunnel in 1900 led to the demise of the remaining through traffic and local shipment dwindled to nothing.

The canal was 'abandoned' by its railway owner in 1944 but was taken into national ownership and then passed to Derbyshire County Council to be given a new lease of life as a leisure artery. Under the County Council, the lower part of the canal is managed as a nature reserve and a lovely one it is, with numerous birds easily spotted, including the kingfisher.

When the next overbridge comes into view, a glance to the left across the River Derwent will reveal the site of a tunnel for the Carsington Reservoir aqueduct. It passes under the canal and river to join the main Derwent Aqueduct on the eastern side of the canal. At the bridge, known as Crich Chase Bridge, leave the towpath and go over the canal. Once over the bridge, turn left along a broad track through a wood and up a walled lane, ignoring the signs saying that it is a private road. It is

Cromford

a public footpath. Follow the lane to a point where it forks and keep right to go over a stile by a metal gate.

Keep straight on now, up a rough lane, which boasts street lights! You emerge eventually from the woodland onto a road at Chasecliff. There is a seat here on the left commanding great views of the Derwent. Cross the road and walk up the lane opposite known as Shaws Hill. The houses here must have magnificent views to the west. Shaws Hill becomes Top Lane and at Hilltop Cottage dips slightly downhill. Keep your eyes peeled here for a narrow path between two houses. It is now signed from the road. If you reach the old pump on the right of the lane you will know that you have gone too far.

Benthill Farm

The path climbs steeply up a flight of steps. At the top, it crosses a narrow walled lane and then continues upward to cross an access track to Benthill Farm. Go straight across the track and through the stile opposite to enter open fields again. The next stile is by a tree stump at the other side of the field and as you reach this, Crich Stand appears reassuringly in view on the left.

In this next field, the path forks and there are two stiles in the far wall. Head for the left hand one which sits to the left of the two trees. Crich church spire now comes into view and is a useful marker for the remainder of the walk. Take a look back here at the magnificent view over the Derwent valley towards Wirksworth.

Assembly Rooms

Continue straight on now with a wall on your right to reach another gap stile by a prominent gate post. In the next field, keep the wall to your left. Derby Assembly Rooms come into sight on the left, but before you think you have gone badly astray remember that this is the old Assembly Rooms frontage which was transferred to Crich Tramway museum to create an authentic street tram image.

Go straight across the next field to a stile slightly to the right of the church. In the next field the path is ahead once again to a gateway in the wall on the right. The bridge which can be seen ahead once carried the path over the Crich Mineral Railway. At this point the line was originally a rope worked incline but was converted to locomotive haulage in 1893 when steam replaced horse power.

Do not go through the gateway but turn left and cross the field again, following a right of way, towards the Tramway Museum and Crich Stand. Locals obviously ignore right of way niceties and cut off this corner. Go through a gateway by a holly tree and to the right of the red brick bungalow thus joining a rough lane which brings you out on the main road almost opposite the Cliff Inn. Then, it is necessary to retrace your steps past Field House and the red brick bungalow bearing left by the holly tree and through the field to the gateway near Church Bridge. Go straight on this time and soon leave the fields to enter Wheatsheaf Lane with houses on either side. Carry on down the lane, bearing right where Jeffreys Lane joins, noting shortly afterwards the excellently preserved stone arched bridge on the left. At the next road junction go left and return to the marketplace.

WALK 9: DARLEY BRIDGE

The Route: Darley Bridge, Oker Hill, Snitterton, Ash Plantation, Wensley, Oldfield Lane. A great short walk on the shoulders of the Derwent valley.

Distance: 3 miles

Start: Picnic Site, Darley Bridge. Map Reference: 270624

Map: Ordnance Survey Outdoor Leisure Map No 24 – The Peak District, White Peak Area

How to get there:

By Bus – There is a bus from Matlock, Bakewell and Chesterfield on Mondays to Saturdays. Alight at the picnic site. On Sundays there is a service along the A6 road to The Whitworth Centre in Darley Dale. It is a ten minute walk to the picnic site from here.

By Car – Travel on the A6 to Darley Dale then on the B5057 to Darley Bridge picnic site.

The Three Stags Head dates back to 1736 according to the lintel above the side door. The lintel also has the carved initials G.O.Q. which were reputedly the initials of the first landlord. The present landlady has a different explanation. Evidently, in those early times the members of the local hunt used to get a little rowdy and at closing time would leave rather noisily. The initials were meant as a reminder to 'Go Out Quietly'. The original stone step used for mounting horses still stands by the inn, presumably dating from a similar period when it would have been a coaching point too.

There are three rooms, a bar, lounge and games room and your hosts Anthony and Patricia Farrell serve a lovely glass of Kimberley ales – Best Mild, Best Bitter and Classic. The landlady was voted Pub Landlady of The Year for the East Midlands Tourist Board Region in 1990 so she knows how to cater well for customers.

The Three Stags Heads is open at lunchtimes except Monday and all day Saturday. Food is served at lunchtimes and by arrangement at early evening as it opens again at 6pm. There is also a very pleasant garden outside suitable for families. In the summer there is often a clog or morris dancing team performing here.

The Walk

From the picnic site, go right along the B5057 road, passing the entrance to Darley Dale Cricket Club founded in 1863. Note the curious wall on the opposite side of the road. This was designed to keep cattle in but let flood water through! Pass the Square and Compass public house which also welcomes hikers. At one time this was Robinson's most easterly outpost. Go over the River Derwent by the splendid mediaeval bridge, noting that all of the arches on the north side are round and, part-way under the arching, the structure seems to change from a smooth arch to a ribbed, pointed one. Mediaeval bridges were usually constructed with pointed arches and because of damage from flood were almost invariably rebuilt on the upstream side. This has happened repeatedly at Darley Bridge and each rebuilding has widened the bridge.

Once over the river, go left along the lane signposted to Oker which is a gated road with little traffic. Go along the lane for a short distance, then go right over a stile onto a path also signed to Oker. Head for the hedge corner by old bath tubs! The route is obvious underfoot, though beyond the baths the field displays remnants of ridge and furrow farming and the furrows are invariably wet.

Oker Hill

The path leaves the field and enters an area of scrub before emerging into a rough lane. Go left here and descend to pass the houses, where the lane becomes no more than a couple of ruts in the grass. At the first gateway past the houses bear right along a narrow path leaving the hedge and track on your left and begin to ascend across the flank of Oker Hill. The tumbled nature of the ground hereabouts is evidence of landslip, for Oker Hill is composed of shales and grits and these are notoriously unstable.

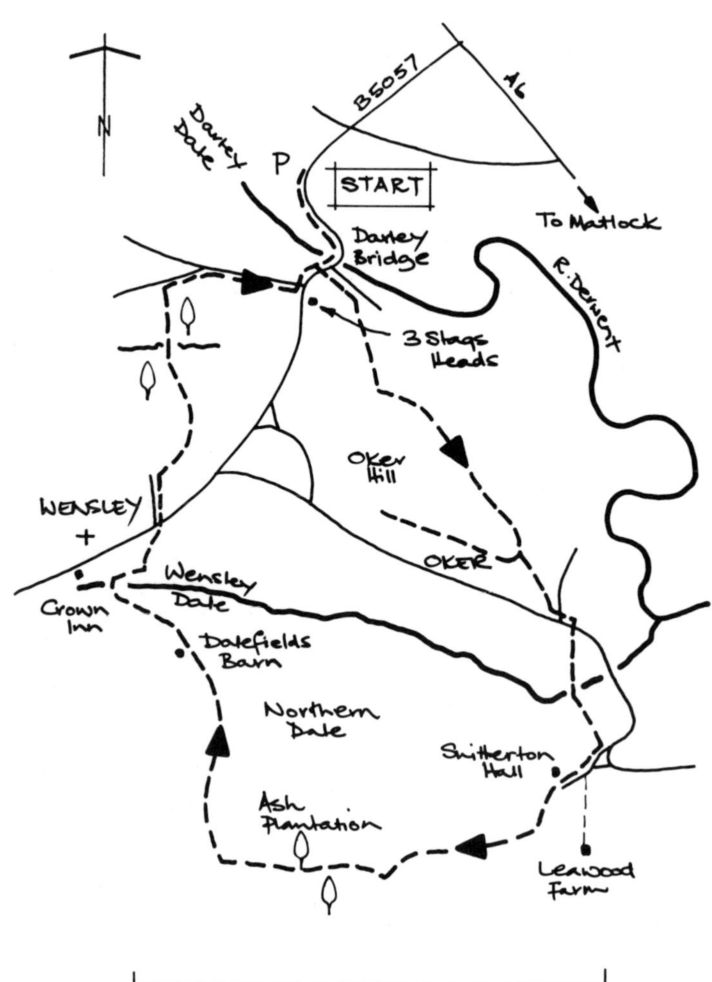
N
B5057
A6
Darley Dale
P
START
To Matlock
Darley Bridge
R. Derwent
3 Stags Heads
Oker Hill
WENSLEY
OKER
Wensley Dale
Crown Inn
Dalefields Barn
Northern Dale
Snitterton Hall
Ash Plantation
Leawood Farm
Scale: 1 mile / 1.6km.

At the first stile, there is a fine view down the valley to Matlock and Riber Castle. At the second the view is less promising for there is a thick growth of scrub. There is a selection of paths tending to the right and upwards. Eventually, they converge on a gateway leading into open fields and another path joins through a gate on the right. Keep straight on here, still climbing to the right to emerge into open hillside. Head for the curious pointed object which looks like the tip of a church steeple but turns out to be a local version of a fence post.

Will Shaw's Tree

Descend towards the derelict barn and pick up an obvious tractor track which slants to the south eastern end of Oker Hill. Here, on the left is a spring known as Graces Well. If you wish to visit the summit of the hill, bear right here and make your way onto the shoulder. Then, go right up the obvious path to the prominent tree which you saw at the start of the walk. This is Will Shaw's Tree and the legend is that the two Shaw brothers said their last goodbyes at this spot, each planting a tree before they departed. One tree alone now flourishes. The legend was put into verse by no lesser poet than Wordsworth.

The summit of the hill lies a little further along the ridge at the trig point where there is an excellent view. Make your way back along the ridge and descend to the track you left earlier. Go right here and follow the track as it drops to a gate just prior to the first houses of Oker village. Go left through a very tight gap stile into a pine wood.

The path through the wood is not too clear so keep to the left hand edge of the wood and soon you emerge into an open field. Do not head for the stile in the left hand corner, but go right, along the edge of the wood towards a drinking trough. A path soon materialises and heads for a seemingly impenetrable hedge, but on close inspection there is a stile which gives out into a lane. Go right here and then left at the T-junction.

Snitterton

In a short distance, there is a stile on the right and an indistinct footpath heads off towards Snitterton. Follow the path with the hedge on the left through a gateway and across a bridge taking you over Wensleydale Brook. Keep straight on across the field, heading for the left hand top corner where there is a signpost. Go over the stile and keep the wall on your left until you meet what looks like a garden gate. It is, but this is the path, tightly constrained between a house on the left and a bungalow on the right. This narrow ginnel soon opens out into a road at the Bull Ring at the centre of Snitterton.

A stone plaque tells of the Bull Ring and there, inset in the road, is the ring itself. Depending on which tale you hear, the ring was either for tethering bulls which were to be baited or were tied there to wait patiently for cows to be brought to them for 'servicing'.

Go right and head up the lane towards Snitterton Hall. Ignore the footpath sign pointing up the driveway to Leawood Farm and continue along the lane, passing the hall on your right. This is a fine Elizabethan building, surrounded by a high stone wall and with its own home farm alongside. The lane ceases as the farmyard is reached, but a track goes off left through a gateway, climbing away up the hillside. Follow this track up the hill to the next gateway where there is a stile. The track continues up the hill but your path lies to the right, up the hollow way following the field wall. This can become overgrown so you may wish to walk along its edge in the field on the left until a stile is reached.

Once over, the hollow way vanishes and so does the path. Ignore the broad green track to your right but instead go sharp left here and climb steeply up to the wall at the top of the field. The path then goes right, along the wall to a tumbledown stile in the wall corner. Ignore the gap in the wall opposite and head up the hill again towards the power lines. In the top left corner of the field is a stile which leads into an ash and hawthorn plantation, known as Ash Plantation. Here, at last the path is obvious and soon becomes cart width as it climbs to leave the wood into open fields.

Continue on the track until it swings left following the electricity line. To the left is Tearsall Mine, originally a lead mine but now being worked as an opencast for fluorspar. Leave the track here and follow a wall on your right, passing by the electricity wires, descending to join another path at a stile in the corner of the field. This is the head of Northern Dale, but there is no path down the dale proper. The path you are on was the miners' path to and from Millclose Mine. The path is clear underfoot, pursuing an unerring course between lead mine shafts (do not venture near) and marked by posts at critical points. At the third stile along this section the path becomes far less clear. However, go left here alongside the wall and come onto the beginnings of a track. Once on the track there is no difficulty and the route passes through another field before Wensley village comes into sight.

Wensley

The track continues easily ahead, passing the monumental Dalesfields Barn and then descending slightly left to drop into the head of Wensleydale. Ignore tracks to the left, but continue down to Wensley-dale Brook then turn right to climb out of the dale again to reach a tarmac road by the first houses of Wensley village. Where the road bends to the left, there is a stile in a wall on the right. This is your route. The Crown Inn, which lay just to the left here, has regretably closed.

Turn right at the stile and descend the footpath around the back of Wensley Hall to emerge on the main road. Immediately opposite is a footpath sign to Birchover and Stanton. It looks like the driveway to a private house but, a short distance along it, there is a stile which you cross to skirt round the right of the house. Where the tarmac ends a narrow green lane goes off right and this is the path. It soon comes into fields and there is a broad way with a hedge on the right and trees to the left. An obvious gateway lies ahead but seek out a stile on the right for this is your route. It is rather like the biblical quote:

'Broad is the way, wide the gate that leadeth to destruction, but straight the way and narrow' . . . the stile that leadeth unto Stanton!

The path descends the field on the right to a point about half way down the left hedge, where there is a stile. Go through this and across the next field to a stile in the far right hand corner. This takes you into a Forestry Commission plantation and onto a broad forest ride which leads downhill. Soon the forest ride turns sharp right and there is a signpost to Oldfield Lane. Follow it as it drops steeply to a stream then rises the last stretch to the lane through new plantations.

Go right here and continue along the road to Darley Bridge, emerging on the main road almost opposite The Three Stags Heads. The way back to the picnic site lies along the main road but bus passengers please note that there is a stop outside the pub!

Darley Bridge

WALK 10: EARL STERNDALE

The Route: Harley Grange, Dowel Dale, Booth Farm, Hollinsclough, Glutton Bridge

Distance: 8 miles

Start: The Quiet Woman, Earl Sterndale. Map Reference: 090670

Map: Ordnance Survey Outdoor Leisure Map No 24 – The Peak District, White Peak Area

How to get there:

By Bus – There is a daily bus service from Buxton to Earl Sterndale or to the village turning on the B5053

By Car – Travel on the B5053 from Brierlow Bar near Buxton or from Bottom House near Leek. The turning to Earl Sterndale is signed from this road.

The Quiet Women at Earl Sterndale is a gem of a pub. It is well liked by locals and those in search of the curious, for the name is most unusual. The inn sign includes the phrase – 'Soft Words Turneth Away Wrath' referring to an earlier landlord who chopped off his wife's head to stop her ranting at him both day and night. Evidently, the village happened to be one hundred percent behind his rather desperate action!

Your present hosts, Kenneth and Jennifer Mellor, serve a very good pint of Marstons Mercian dark mild, Burton bitter and Pedigree. It is difficult to leave this friendly pub once you are settled, so we suggest that you do the walking first and adjourn later. It is the sort of pub where there is no need for a juke box but there is occasional impromptu live music as musicians and folk singers call in. Whilst there has been a considerable amount of renovation this has been done in a very sympathetic manner including the restoration of natural beams and the building of a limestone grate.

The pub also offers a range of bar snacks available including prized Wardles' pork pies from Buxton. The pub is usually open at lunchtimes throughout the week and at 6 pm in the evenings especially in the summer. If trade is sufficient, the pub stays open all day.

There are seats outside The Quiet Woman and around the garden are bantams, ducks and geese so the children love it. The landlord also hopes to add an aviary.

Across the village green is Earl Sterndale church, the only rural church in Derbyshire to be the target of a bomb during the last war. It must have been mistaken for a strategic target. The surrounding village is very much a working community, most people being involved in agriculture or quarrying on the other side of the hill.

The Walk

From the entrance to The Quiet Woman, turn left on the road and follow this as it descends gently to a crossroads at the top of Glutton Dale. Cross over and walk along the road signed to Axe Edge. The road climbs gently and bends to the left before approaching a farm, Harley Grange. Turn left along the track before the farm and follow this as it dips then rises to up to a gate. Go through it and the next gate on the right and then left to cross a stile with the footpath signed to Dowel Dale.

Keep walking ahead and this quiet narrow dale comes into view across the field. Cross the stile and the path plunges down to another stile and onto the road. Go right and walk up the dale. Pass by Owl Hole, presumably the haunt of the nocturnal creature but unfortunately full of rubbish. The road sweeps around onto open ground and to the left of Greensides Farm. It continues to rise but before the yellow grit box look for a turning on your left. Follow this for a short distance, cross a stile and as the track leads away left to Stoop Farm go right, follow the sign to Booth Farm. Go through a gateway and head for the road, through another gap and then over a stile, Booth Farm being down the track on your left.

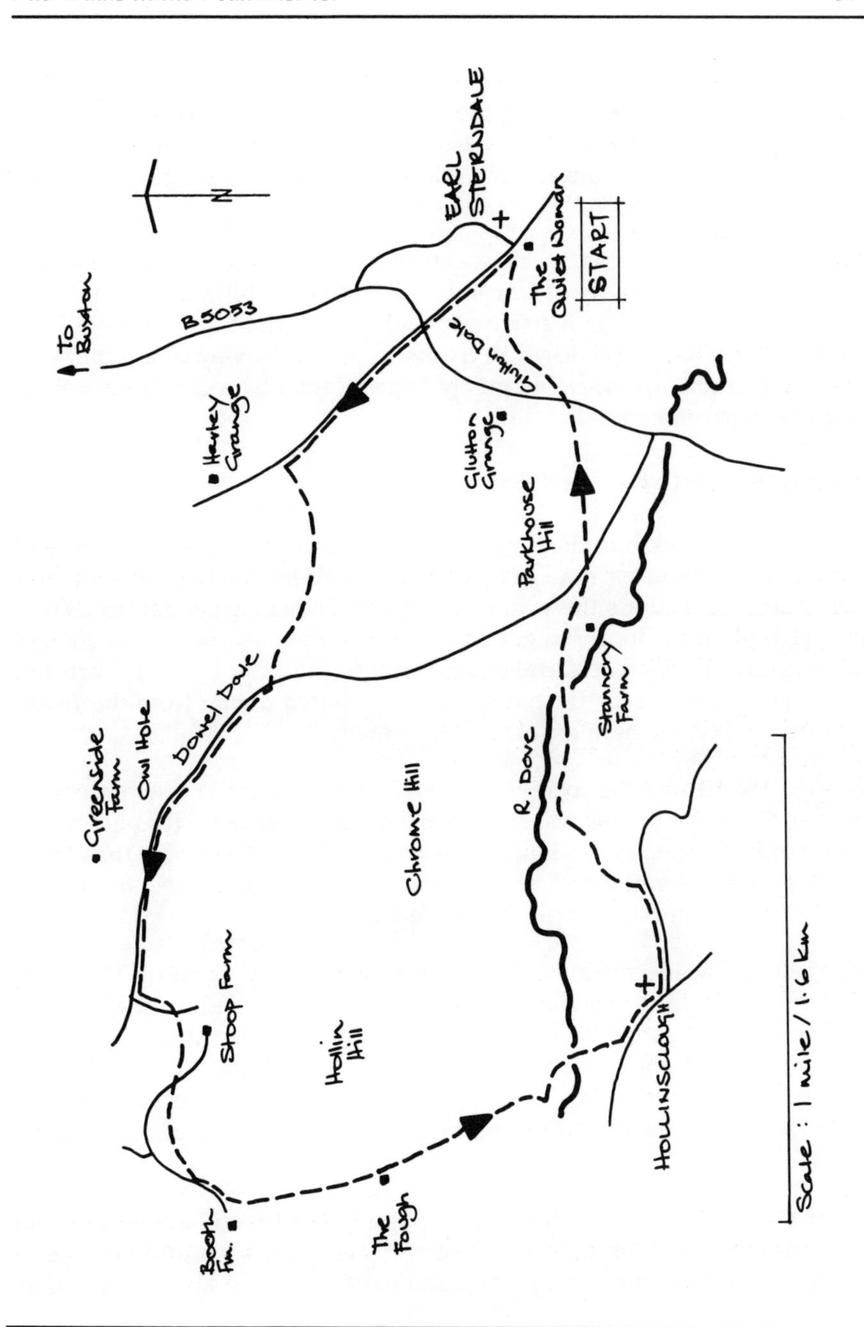
N
To Buxton
B5053
EARL STERNDALE
The Quiet Woman
START
Glutton Dale
Glutton Grange
Parkhouse Hill
Stannery Farm
Dowel Dale
Owl Hole
Greenside Farm
Chrome Hill
R. Dove
Stoop Farm
Hollin Hill
HOLLINSCLOUGH
The Fough
Booth Fm.
Scale : 1 mile / 1.6 km

Turn left along the access road to the farm but when it forks take the left track through a gateway along the edge of beautiful valley in the lee of Hollins Hill. This descends to pass a house known as The Fough, on your right. Continue ahead but when the track forks again take the lower track down the valley.

The green track begins to curve around the hillside towards Hollins Farm, with superb views of Chrome and Parkhouse hills. Leave the track at this corner to follow a narrower path to the right shown by a blue waymarker. This drops down to cross the stream by way of a footbridge and then climbs up the bank, gently left and then by a drystone wall to exit at a gate onto a road.

Hollinsclough

Turn left and walk into the hamlet of Hollinsclough, a classic example of rural depopulation for it no longer has its post office, school or shop and rarely sees a bus. Pass the water trough and Bethel chapel dating 1801, a chapel built by a local 'jaggerman', John Lomas. A jaggerman looked after teams of packhorses travelling through the Peak District. Turn left at the junction to go by the old school and church dating from the 1840s, probably when the hamlet was still in growth.

Beyond the hamlet the road curves left and then right at a wider corner by a ford. Leave the tarmac road by walking ahead here, through a gap stile next to a gate, and along a track through the fields. Go through a gateway on the right and at the junction go left as signed to cross a footbridge by the ford across the infant Dove.

Keep ahead at the main path and pass by Stannery Farm on the right, through a stile by a gateway. Come to a tarmac lane and walk along this for 50 paces or so before striking off slightly left opposite a stile in the wall on the right. Proceed slightly left across the field, and not immediately left towards a white marker on the left. Cross a stile by a gate and walk straight on to another stile by a gate and ahead to cross the B5053 road.

Once over cross another stile and go slightly left up and across the field to go through a stone gap stile. The path then turns left and becomes a steep climb as it curves right and then left to a stile above marked in yellow. You'll need to pause here to catch your breath, but the view down Glutton Dale is exhilarating. Walk ahead to another gap stile by a gateway and then go slightly right across a field heading in the direction of Earl Sterndale church. This leads you through a couple stiles to a narrow path behind a cottage to the Quiet Woman public house.

WALK 11: ELTON

The Route: Elton, Anthony Hill, Cliff Farm, Harthill Moor, Robin Hoods Stride, Dudwood Lane

Distance: 2 to 3 miles

Start: The Duke of York, Elton. Map Reference: 229613

Map: Ordnance Survey Outdoor Leisure Map No 24 – The Peak District, White Peak Area.

How to get there:

By Bus – There is a daily bus except Sundays from Matlock, Bakewell and Chesterfield.

By Car – From the A6 travel on the B5056 from Piccory Corner or from the A5012 at Grangemill to Elton cross roads then follow the signs to Elton. Another route is by way of the B5057 from the A6 at Darley Dale via Winster to Elton cross roads. There is limited on-street car parking in Elton, so please park considerately.

Elton's pub is the Duke of York which serves Mansfield beers but unfortunately has no real ale at present. It is an old fashioned pub with separate rooms where village chat goes on. The pub does not serve food and is not open lunchtimes except on Sundays. Evening opening is from 8 pm onwards. Nevertheless, this unspoilt local is well worth a visit.

If it is closed, the nearest pubs are in Winster – see Ramble 28.

The Walk

Go down Well Street, to the left of the church. At the fork in the lane bear left. It is signed to Youlgreave. At the gate at the end of the lane go into the fields and turn left to the hedge and then right. Descend the field which is the site of the Elton ski tow in Winter and and at the bottom, proceed through the right-hand stile. The prominent rocky outcrop ahead is Anthony Hill.

The path is clearly in view ahead. It dips to a small stream then ascends to a stile by a solitary hawthorn. Bear right here to clip the corner of the field. There is a good view to Birchover and Winster from this point. The path continues diagonally across the field, heading steadily uphill to a stile in the top corner by the red gate. The next field again has its corner clipped, an indication that the path pre-dates the field boundaries and

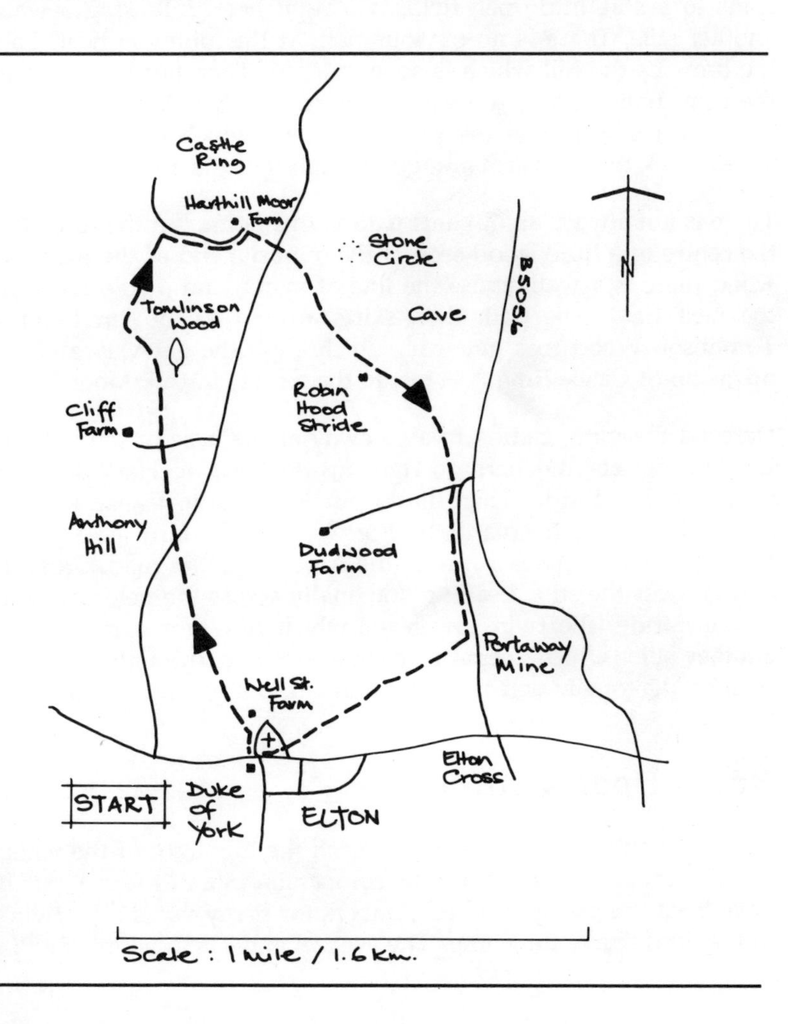

was of sufficient importance to retain its original line at the time of enclosure. In his research into the route of the ancient Derbyshire Portway, the late Richard Cockerton speculated that the prehistoric route may well have followed this alignment, as it keeps to higher ground, rather than following the later, well-documented route down to Dudwood Lane and by Robin Hood's Stride.

The path crosses a final field to emerge on the road at a stile. Cross the road and take the signed path to Youlgreave. A short scrubby stretch leads to a stile into open fields. Go right here, following a wall up to another stile. There is no obvious path at this point so head boldly for the brow of the hill which is soon reached. Then head for a gateway at the right hand end of the wall, with Youlgreave clearly in view ahead. There is a stile just to the left of the gate which you cross. Cross the access track to Cliff Farm and go through the stile ahead.

There is not always an obvious path at this point, but the route heads for the centre of a little wood seen at the opposite end of the field. Near the wood there is a wall across the line of march and a stile takes you into the next field. The path then skirts around to the left hand side of Tomlinson Wood to a gateway. Go through the gateway and the view opens up of Castle Ring Fort just to the left of Harthill Moor Farm.

Descend the path leading to a gateway at the base of the hill on which Castle Ring sits and here go right up the track to Harthill Moor Farm signed to The Stride. There is no public access to Castle Ring, an Iron Age hillfort built to guard the Portway. At the farm go right and the farm access soon gives out onto the Alport to Elton road. Cross the road and go over the stile, heading diagonally across the field towards Robin Hoods Stride, the twin towers of which now come into view. Cross another stile, which seems to change position from time to time, and then go diagonally across the field again to a gateway to the left of the Stride.

Robin Hood's Stride

Go over a stile near the gate and reach the highlight of the walk, Robin Hoods Stride. The Stride and its companion pile of rocks, Cratcliffe Tor, have been the playground of climbers for many years. The twin towers of the Stride have the names The Weazel and The Inaccessible Pinnacles.

Please note that the MWS who carved his name so deeply in The Weazel is not one of the authors of this book! Apart from the two pinnacles, the summit rocks of the Stride are an easy scramble and offer magnificent views.

Despite the name, this has been an important landmark and routeway from the earliest times. To the north lies the Iron Age hillfort of Castle Ring and the Harthill Moor stone circle. Below the Stride was a Romano-British settlement, while on the flat land between The Stride and Cratcliffe Tor was a small village surrounded by a ditch and palisade. The ditch can still be seen. On the southern slopes of the Tor is the Hermit's Cave, sheltered by two ancient yew trees. The cave still has a sleeping bench and a carved crucifix, while on the rock walls outside there are channels in the stone to guide water away from the cave into containers. The hermit apparently gave succour to the weary travellers

The Duke of York, Elton (courtesy of Chris Rushton, Evening Sentinel)

who had hurried to this spot in the mistaken belief that they were approaching the lights of a great house at dusk. From a distance the Stride does give the impression of being a building and in earlier times was known as Mock Beggars Hall.

Leave the Stride with reluctance and head southwards down the cart track between it and Cratcliffe Tor, to emerge onto a road near to a stream. To your left is the 'new' road, an eighteenth century turnpike route. Ahead is Dudwood Lane, at one time part of the Portway. Go ahead up Dudwood Lane, passing Dudwood Farm.

A short way beyond the farm where the climb steepens there is a stile on the right. Go through this and into open fields, heading slightly left across the field, up the hill towards the spoil heaps. The path is not always distinct but skirts around the head of some rocky outcrops to come to the back of a playing field. A track on the left leads directly back to the main street in Elton but continue on, over a stile. The path descends quite sharply before rising again, passing a waymarker post to emerge on a back lane by the church yard. The path continues through the churchyard to the main street opposite the Duke of York.

WALK 12: GREAT LONGSTONE

The Route: Longstone Edge and return. A climb up to the edge, offering superb views across The Peak District.

Distance: 3 miles

Start: The White Lion. Map Reference: 199718

Map: Ordnance Survey Outdoor Leisure Map No 24 – The Peak District, White Peak Area

How to get there:

By Bus – There is a Monday to Saturday service from Bakewell.

By Car – Travel on the A6020 from Ashford in the Water and turn left as signed. There is limited on street car parking in the village.

Step up off the street into The White Lion at Great Longstone and you'll find a boot scraper and a notice welcoming walkers with or without their boots on! This two roomed pub is very friendly and your hosts Glenys and Brian Marshall do their best to make the walker feel at ease. The home cooking and tasty Robinson beers help. They offer Best Mild and Best Bitter on electric pump in the two rooms, a bar to the left and a lounge and restaurant area on the right.

For those who fancy a coffee before starting their ramble, it is served from 1030 onwards and the bar opens at 1130 for the lunch session and at 6 pm which is useful for a summer's evening ramble. This is a pub which caters for the rambler.

Great Longstone is one of the more traditional villages in the area, not much affected by the large number of visitors coming into the Peak District. The houses nestled about the green with village cross are mainly of stone but Longstone Hall stands as a red brick building of considerable character. Besides quarrying and farming this area was also at one time a small centre of stocking manufacture but this has long since gone. Unusually, there is another Robinson's pub in the village called The Crispin.

The Walk

From The White Lion, go slightly left across the road to walk up a narrow way to the churchyard. Go through the kissing gate and through the peaceful environs of this lovely church. Note the restored church cross. The path exits onto a lane. Walk along it for a short distance before turning left along a rough track.

Keep ahead until a gap stile is reached by a gate and then cross the field slightly right to cross another gap stile. Continue in the same direction to another gap stile and then walk up the dry valley. At the top end, go left over a gap stile by a gate. The path climbs the gentle slope of this field

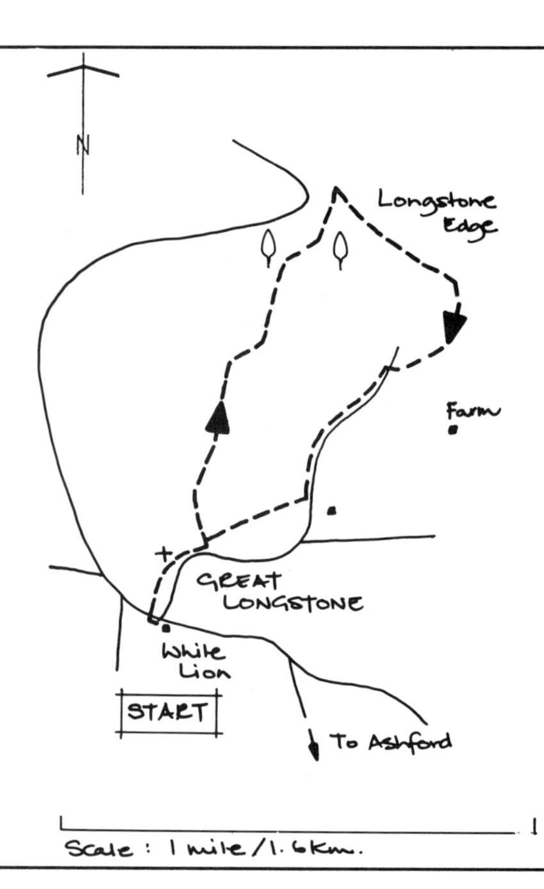

heading for a stile which exits onto a steeper slope. Pause here and look over to the Wye valley and to Magpie Mine near Sheldon, one feature of the Ashford walk.

The path now climbs slightly right up the hill between patches of scrub, to join a main track along the edge. Go right here, to dip at first but then to climb a little further before turning right as signed. The path is not clear at first as it slants down the slope. However, it soon widens and becomes more prominent between the hawthorns. It eventually reaches a drystone wall and here you cross a high level stile into a field. Head slightly right across the field towards the far right corner. At the drystone wall go through a gap stile into a narrower enclosure. Cross the stile by a gate and the path into a narrow lane which winds its way left, then right and left. Farm buildings can be seen ahead and it is important to be vigilant for you have to cross a gap stile on the right along this section of lane.

Once through the stile, keep ahead in this long narrow field to pass through two gap stiles. Proceed ahead along a track to join the one used on the outward journey. Turn left and at the road right. Follow this back into Great Longstone. More than likely you will find eggs and other produce on sale here as well as a dairy in the village offering milk. Pass by the old forge and Social Institute. The rural economy still thrives!

WALK 13: HULME END

The Route: Manifold Trail, Dale Bridge, Warslow. A short ramble but with one steep climb.

Distance: 5 miles

Start: The Car Park at Hulme End old railway station. Map Reference: 103594

Map: Ordnance Survey Outdoor Leisure Map No 24 – The Peak District, White Peak Area

How to get there:

By Bus – There are daily buses from Buxton and an infrequent service from Leek.

By Car – Travel on the B5054 from the A515 Buxton to Ashbourne road or on the B5053 Brierlow Bar to Bottom House road, turning at Warslow onto the B5054. There is a designated car park at Hulme End.

The Greyhound at Warslow is a lovely pub with a tap room, games room and lounge. It serves Theakstons XB and draught Bass on hand pull and offers an extensive menu; a favourite of the authors being a ploughman's which includes locally produced White Stilton from Hartington.

The inn has served weary travellers for many years, being on the Leek to Buxton coaching route and the longer distance pilgrimage routes of earlier centuries. A few years back a guest at the inn was a spiritualist who saw a ghost of a young serving maid dating from the eighteenth century. The landlady has seen her too, sitting by the fire late at night in the lounge bar in a very quiet and non threatening manner. Not that all Warslow's ghosts are so subdued for legend has it that a headless horseman rides up and down the village from time to time. Could this be the same ghost that rides the pastures of Butterton Moor? Keep supping the ale and the story becomes more believable.

The Greyhound is open from 11.30 until 2.30 pm in the summer and from 6 pm in the evening. In the winter it opens at 12 noon and at 7 pm again in the evenings. You can be assured of a warm welcome.

The Greyhound Inn, Warslow (courtesy of Chris Rushton, Evening Sentinel)

The Manifold Valley Hotel, formerly the Light Railway, in Hulme End serves Wards beers and good food in a friendly atmosphere. It has seats outside and opens lunchtimes throughout the week.

The Walk

The walk starts at the car park at the head of the Manifold Trail, a virtually car free route down the Manifold valley. This was once the northern terminus of the Manifold Valley Light Railway, a most unusual affair and, in effect, a narrow gauge extension of The North Staffordshire railway from Leekbrook Junction and Waterhouses. The little railway was opened as late as 1904 and closed in 1934, not surprisingly as it ran from nowhere to nowhere. Amazingly, the then county council safeguarded it for future leisure purposes – including the old station buildings which can still be seen. The station used to be called 'Hulme End – for Sheen and Hartington' even though by this time Hartington had its very own station on another line. Until 1993, a railway service was provided during a few weekends in July from Hulme End along a short stretch of line into The Manifold, with proceeds going to charity.

From the car park, walk along the Manifold Trail which curves between the steeply sided valley with Ecton Hill to your left, at one time mined for copper ore. The Duke of Devonshire made considerable sums from this and invested his wealth heavily in the re development of Buxton in Georgian times, including the building of the impressive Crescent.

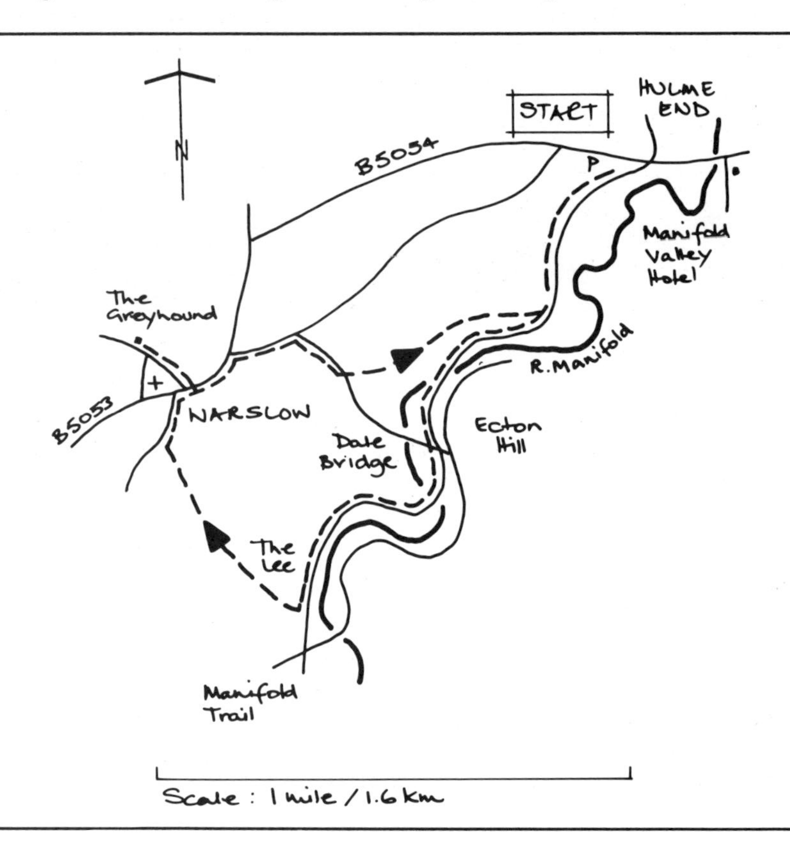

Dale Bridge

Cross the road at Dale Bridge then over the River Manifold, continuing along the trail – a wooded section, verges thick with thistle, campion and cow parsley. The track comes to a gate and road. Take the path up to the right to cross a stile. Go right and begin to climb up the bank. Be vigilant for there is a little stone gap stile on the left in the hedge. Go through it and turn right, continuing up the slope once again. Go through another gap stile, then head slightly left towards a derelict barn.

Cross another stile and walk ahead to a gap stile adjacent to a gate. The village of Warslow comes into view as you progress through wet ground to the very top of the field. To the left you can see in the distance the spires of Grindon and Butterton churches. Go through the gateway and turn right. This track leads to the main B5053 road. Warslow looks very much like a moorland village with its stone buildings belonging to an estate. The church is in a central position. It dates from the 1820s but with stained glass of a later age very much in the *art nouveau* fashion.

The name *Werslei* was mentioned in the Domesday book and this has since been corrupted to Warslow. The village owes its existence predominantly to agriculture and this remains true to this day. Turn left at the next junction for the short detour to The Greyhound. Then retrace your steps back to the B road and turn left. Pass by the old village stores complete with petrol pump in the forecourt.

At the next junction go right and then soon afterwards right again. As the lane comes to a corner, go ahead through a gateway. Keep to the left hand hedge at first but then as it bends sharp left walk in a gentler curve between hawthorns at the top of the bank. Keep ahead with the hedge and wall to your left, descending gently along the slope. As the field opens up on the left and in the line with the old buildings on Ecton hill opposite, go through a stone gap stile. You should also be able to see the copper spire of an unusual house built in the 1930s by local MP, Arthur Ratcliffe.

The path begins to drop as you walk between ash and elder and then into a narrow green pasture. Keep ahead and the path eventually drops more sharply to a signpost and then right for a short section to exit onto the Manifold Trail once again. Turn left for Hulme End.

WALK 14: LITTON

The Route: Litton, Cressbrook, Cressbrookdale, Tansley Dale. A superb walk with dramatic descents and climbs so it is more than a gentle stroll.

Distance: 5 to 6 miles

Start: The Red Lion, Litton. Map Reference: 164753

Map: Ordnance Survey Outdoor Leisure Map No 24 – The Peak District, White Peak Area.

How to get there:

By Bus – There is a daily bus between Chesterfield and Manchester calling at Litton.

By Car – Travel on the A623 road between Barmoor Clough and Baslow. Turn off for Litton at The Anchor inn, near Tideswell or at the turning near Wardlow Mires. There is a limited amount of on street car parking in the village.

The Red Lion at Litton is a splendid place to eat, for in many respects it is more of a restaurant than a public house. The Boddingtons beer is good and the atmosphere pleasant but the emphasis is definitely on the food. It is very rarely open at lunch except for a short time at weekends.. It is not open Monday evenings.

Given this, it might be better to call into Tideswell after the ramble to The George Hotel, a roomy eighteenth century coaching inn which serves an exceptionally good pint of Kimberley ales, having Mild, Bitter and Classic on handpull at a central bar serving three rooms adjacent to it. The beer should be good for the George has won the local CAMRA branch 'pub of the month' award on more than one occasion.

Having sampled one or two glasses, you might like to try the 'Test Your Reaction' machine on the wall, a hand grip which indicates on a meter how quickly you are responding to a situation! There are also press button bells on the walls to call for waiter service but they are not in use these days. This is a busy inn catering for both locals and guests. It is open lunchtimes throughout the week, serves food and is centrally situated in the village for bus stops and car parking.

The Walk

Start the walk from the Red Lion at Litton. Turn left to join the main road, cross it and turn next right down another road. At the first right hand corner go left into a track, but then immediately right to cross a stile into a field. At the bottom of this field cross a stile and then proceed slightly left heading for another stile which you cross. Continue to climb this next field to a gap stile. Cross the track and go over a stone stile to enter another field. Go through two further stiles and narrow enclosures in roughly the same direction now heading for a gap ahead, still climbing this plateau.

Cressbrookdale

Head for a gap stile to the left of a gate in the left corner. Keep ahead to a wooden stile and cross it to enter the wood above Cressbrookdale. Go right here and be very careful for the path soon drops precipituously left and then right to join another track below. This runs down to join a path coming in from the left. At the stile there is a choice. If you wish to see Cressbrook Mill, then continue to the road corner and follow the lower road down to the mill. If not, turn left to go over the stile and follow the route mentioned at the bottom of the next paragraph. Cressbrook Mill is a splendid building, the original being built by Richard Arkwright. The building seen today dates mainly from 1815 and has served as a textile mill. The restoration of the mill is being actively pursued but is proving very difficult. Its fate has not been finally decided – some saying that it will be a timeshare complex, others that it will become a hotel.

At Cressbrook Mill retrace your steps up the road signed to Litton and begin to climb up the hill. Pass the sign to Ravensdale and as the road bends sharp left continue ahead into the wood. Exit in a short distance by a stile onto a track above the Cress Brook. Keep company with the wall on the right as you descend more sharply to a footbridge across the stream.

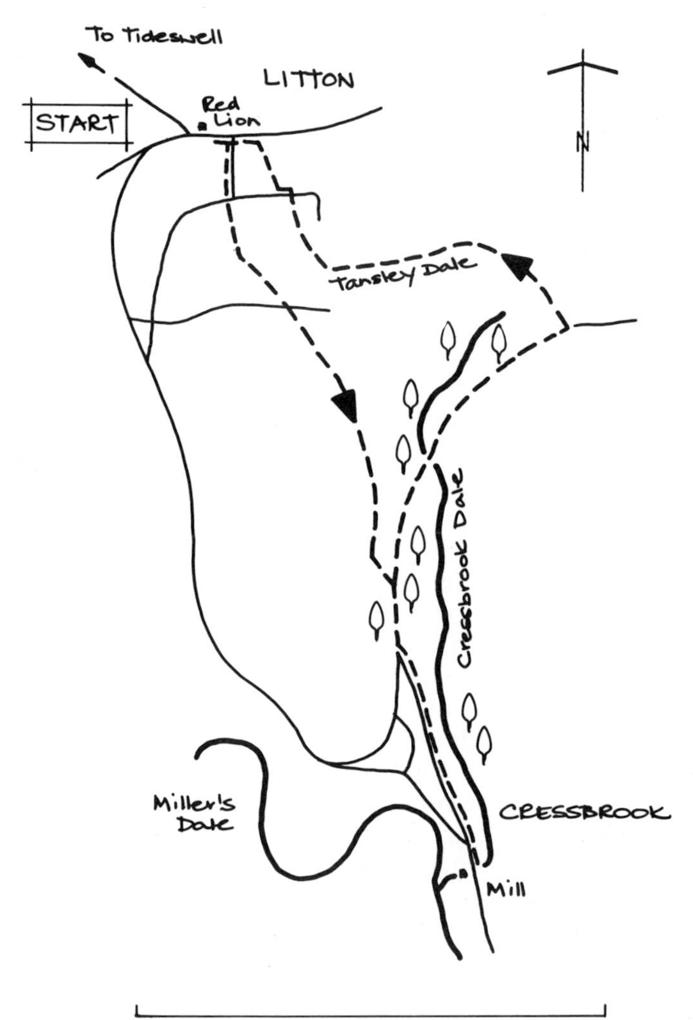
To Tideswell
LITTON
START
Red Lion
N
Tansley Dale
Cressbrook Dale
Miller's Dale
CRESSBROOK
Mill
Scale : 1 mile / 1.6 Km.

Breathtaking

The climbing begins for the path is something of a goat track up the side of the dale. Keep climbing, avoiding any lower paths, until you reach the summit by a gully. The views up the dale are breathtaking, making the hard slog worthwhile. Go left to descend once again into the dale. Follow the well trodden path up the dale until it begins to narrow before curving right.

Tansley Dale

At this point go left to cross a stile and enter Tansley Dale, a much smaller and narrower dale. Soon your path exits at the head of the dale climbing up to the right, with a drystone wall on your left, to a ladder stile. Cross it and follow the drystone wall on the right to a corner. Walk up to the narrow slip of field towards Litton. Cross a stile to join a track and then go left. Within a hundred paces look for a stone stile on the right. Cross it and then the field diagonally to exit by a cottage onto the main road in Litton.

WALK 15: LONGNOR

The Route: Longnor, Beggar's Bridge, Crowdecote, Pilsbury, Over Boothlow

Distance: 10 miles

Start: Longnor Square. Map Reference: 088648

Map: Ordnance Survey Outdoor Leisure Map No 24 – The Peak District, White Peak Area.

How to get there:

By Bus – There is a daily bus service from Buxton. On Sundays, Bakers 'Moorland Rider' serves Longnor from The Potteries and Buxton.

By Car – Travel on the B5053 from Brierlow Bar near Buxton or from Bottom House near Leek. There is car parking in the square.

The Packhorse at Crowdecote is aptly named for in years gone by it would have served many a weary 'jaegar' or 'jagger', the men who looked after trains of packhorses on their journey through the Peak District. The present publicans have lived in the area for some time and look after both local and visitor trade in a welcoming manner. The pub which is open at lunchtimes and evenings throughout the week, serves a range of brews including Boddingtons, Burton ale and Timothy Taylor's Landlord, the latter being unusual for these parts. It also offers bar meals at lunchtimes. The stuffed oatcakes are gorgeous.

The pub has two separate areas around a central bar and often has an open fire in winter to warm the soul and body. The entrance is on the right of the pub from the car park rather than the front door and it is easy enough to kick off dirty boots here. The pub is open from noon until 2 pm in the winter but in the summer opens much longer and all day if people are about. It reopens at 7 pm in winter. If the timing of your walk means that you wish to call into a pub at Longnor on return from the walk, there are plenty of pubs to choose from but the Horseshoes is very welcoming.

Some say that Longnor is a place for longevity for, in the churchyard behind the Market Square, lies the grave of one time resident William Billinge who lived in the seventeenth and part of the eighteenth centuries to reach the ripe old age of 112. What is surprising is his epitaph which cites his career in the army, and the battles he participated in at home and abroad. The words on his gravestone read:

Billited by death,
I quartered here remain
When the trumpet sounds
I'll rise and March again.'

The Walk

From the Market Square of Longnor, a scene almost reminiscent of a Thomas Hardy novel, turn left and walk past the Cheshire Cheese public house, and then to a group of cottages known as Town End. Just beyond these, turn left and walk up a track which bends to the left to a point called Top o'th' Edge. What a splendid view there is from here, across the pastures of the Dove to unusual looking hills with equally strange names of Aldery, Hitter and Chrome, dramatic limestone formations contrasting with the gritstone edge of Longnor.

Beggar's Bridge

Walk down the hillside on a worn path to a barn, which stands to the left of Longnor's sewerage plant. A pace or so beyond the barn turn right as the path leads away over wet ground, rising at first then head slightly left to Beggar's Bridge, spanning the River Dove. Names such as this are intriguing for one wonders whether there would have been beggars at the bridge in past times, or does it refer to thieves laying in wait as packhorse trains approached. Longnor certainly played a key role in earlier times as a marketplace to this part of North Staffordshire and many a farmer would have come to market this way. Longnor's old town hall, dating from 1873, is evidence of its previous importance. It is now a used to produce and sell crafts. Take a look at the tablet over the doorway when you return.

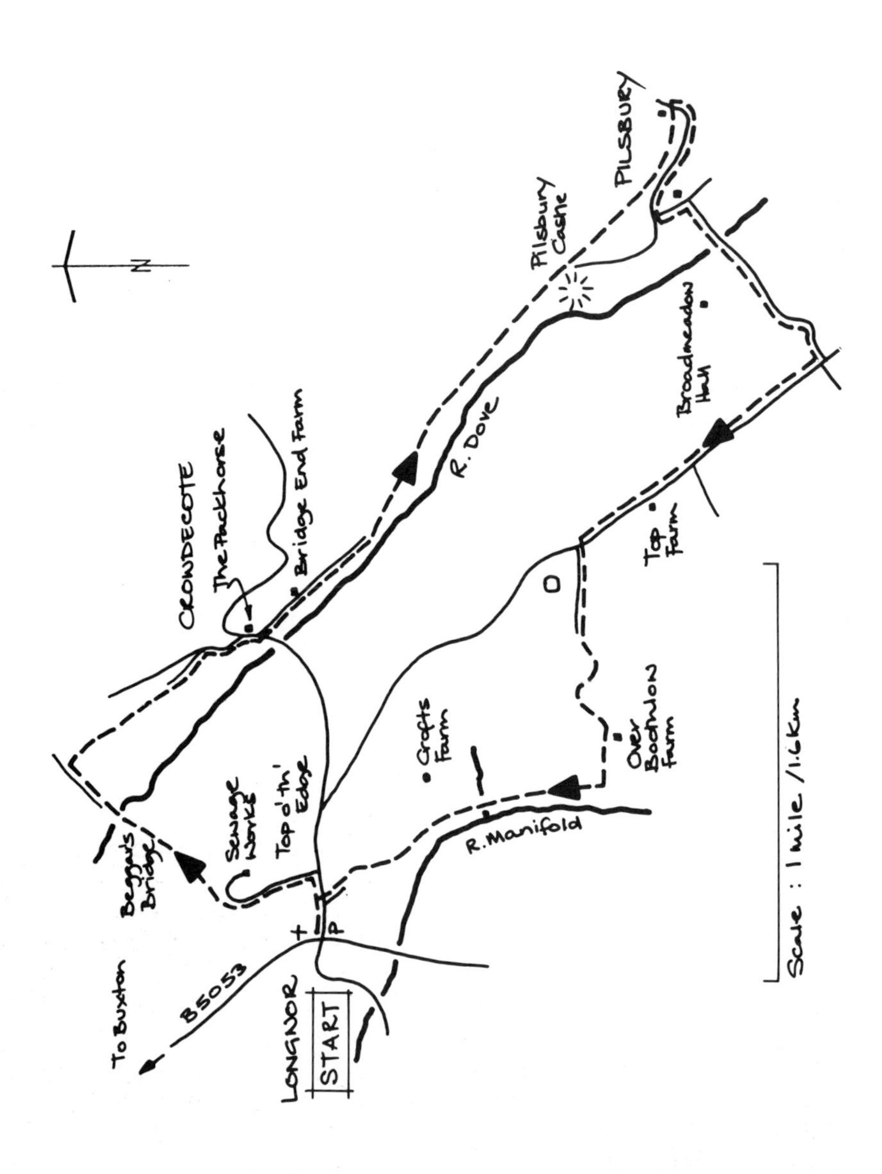
N
PILSBURY
Pilsbury Castle
Broadmeadow Hall
R. Dove
Bridge End Farm
The Packhorse
CROWDECOTE
Top Farm
Over Boothlow Farm
Crofts Farm
Top o' th' Edge
Sewage Works
R. Manifold
Beggar's Bridge
To Buxton
B5053
P
LONGNOR
START
Scale : 1 mile / 1.6 Km

Crowdecote

Cross into Derbyshire and the path soon meets a wider track. However, bear right here across a stile and in a very short distance a ladder stile. Continue ahead, a fence and then a hedge to your left. The path widens to become a track, passing by a farm and into the hamlet of Crowdecote. Turn right at the tarmac road to reach The Pack Horse public house.

If not imbibing pass by the two snug cottages on the road and turn left along a track towards Bridge End Farm. However, at the fork in the track bear right and keep ahead to squeeze by the barred gate (rather than turning right down to the bridge). You will often put a grey heron to flight here, seeing it glide gently into the air above the Dove. Follow the track alongside a drystone wall for two fields, coming to a point where there is an option of two gates. Take the right hand gate and walk the short section of tree lined track before going through a gap stile by a

Walking in the Upper Dove

gateway. The track now becomes a path, still keeping ahead mid field. Cross a track and sheep pens and now Pilsbury Castle comes into view.

Pilsbury Castle

Set in such an isolated place, this monument is important, for it is one of Derbyshire's finest surviving motte and bailey mounds. This would not have been a castle built predominantly of stone such as Peveril, but more of a wooden palisade, with a tower and other buildings. However, in this instance no lord chose to re build this fortress completely in stone. There is little or no evidence to suggest that it was used for fortification beyond the fourteenth century.

Cross another stile into the next field and then the path passes through a stile by a gateway and keeps to the left of the mound as it rises. Cross the stile on the left and look at the information board on you right. There is a choice here. Many walkers follow the path on the right down to Pilsbury hamlet. However, for better views climb up the hillside slightly left but continuing ahead as signed. It comes to a drystone wall which you cross in the corner and then through another stile once through a small enclosure, to cut slightly left across the field to exit onto the lane by the barn.

Turn right and follow the road right down to the farm, cows eating contentedly to Radio One in the milking shed, and once through the barred gate turn right down to a bridge across the river. Once over, follow the old track ahead up the hill to the tarmac lane. You might have glimpsed the distinctive looking house, Broadmeadow Hall, on your right. Note also Sheen Hill beyond, a formidable looking rise.

Turn right on the road and follow this for half a mile, beyond the turning for Brund and Ridge End. Pass Top Farm on the left and not far after as you approach a building and a water reservoir on the left. Turn left along a track after the lay-by. This leads to a junction where you keep ahead into a field with an old quarry scar on the right. Walk down the hill with the drystone wall to your left. As you approach a corner with recently planted trees, cut right as the tractor track does, to the gateway and once through turn left to cross the field in the direction of Over Boothlow Farm. The track descends gently to a gate which you go through and then turn right by the buildings to go through another gate into a large farmyard area with the farmhouse ahead. Turn right and go through a gap stile by the barred gate leading onto the farm drive.

The Manifold

Follow the farm drive towards the River Manifold but before reaching it go right along an obvious path, which follows through two fields before sweeping left closer to the river banks. Cross the small bridge over a tributary and keep ahead as the river curves left. The temptation is to follow the river bank but as the village of Longnor appears on your right look for the path which curves away right through the field towards the buildings.

Go through a stile and continue upwards, heading slightly left to a stile next to a barn. This brings you into a farmyard often with yapping dogs. Bear right on to a road which leads up to a junction where you turn left for the Market Square.

The Packhorse Inn, Crowdecote (courtesy of Chris Rushton, Evening Sentinel)

WALK 16: MIDDLETON BY WIRKSWORTH

Route: Black Rocks, Cromford Incline, Birchwood, Wigwellbrook, Bole Hill, National Stone Centre, Middleton, Steeple Grange

Distance: 3 – 4 miles

Start: The Car Park at Black Rocks (Bus stop nearby). Map Reference: 282550

Map: Ordnance Survey Outdoor Leisure Map No 24 – The Peak District, White Peak Area.

How to get there:

By Bus – Daily buses from Bakewell, Matlock and Derby

By Car – Travel on the B5023 from Duffield to Wirksworth then on the B5036 to Black Rocks car park. Alternatively, travel on the A6 to Cromford and then the B5036 where the car park is signed from the B5035/5036 junction.

Frank and Hazel Ryan run a cheerful pub, the Rising Sun at Middleton by Wirksworth, a stone built house of character where walkers are always very welcome. It was at one time a pub cum farm and still retains a small amount of land. It is usually open at lunchtimes between 1130 and 2.30 pm, opening again for the evening at 7 pm. On offer is a champion beer, Ind Coope Burton Ale as well as Tetley Bitter, both served by hand pull. Bar snacks, lunches and evening meals are also served and the landlady likes to use only the freshest of produce whenever possible. Accommodation is also available at the inn.

According to the locals one of the inn's bedrooms is haunted by the ghost of a small child. In the 1950s the then landlord, who is now a regular customer, lived on the premises without knowing that there was a secret bedroom boarded up. It was only after he left that he became aware of its existence by observing the position of an external window.

After some discussion, the new landlord broke through an internal wall and discovered an empty double bedroom with no explanation of why the room had been sealed off. The mystery remains for the Ryans have not encountered a ghost in this room; but after a pint or two of Burton Ale who knows!

The Walk

Leave Black Rocks car park and follow the signs onto the High Peak Trail. Turn left along the trail. This was once the Cromford and High Peak railway, opened in 1830 and closed in 1967. Built using canal technology with long flat stretches and steep inclines in place of locks, the line linked the Peak Forest and Cromford canals. On the opening of the Matlock to Buxton line in the 1860s the Cromford and High Peak lost its *raison d'etre* as a through route but served a plethora of private sidings, mainly quarries which kept it in business until the 1960s.

Black Rocks was once a gritstone quarry, but many lead mines were sunk, piercing the gritstone to reach the ore bearing limestone tens of feet beneath. The views from the trail at this point over Matlock Gorge to Riber and Willersley castles are superb. The latter castle was built for Richard Arkwright, of Spinning Jenny fame, who had established highly profitable mills at Cromford. The castle is now a Methodist church holiday centre and the mills are in the care of the Arkwright Society. There is also a heritage centre open to the public.

Sheep Pasture Incline

The trail soon reaches the top of Sheep Pasture incline. On the right is the reservoir and remains of the engine house. This engine, built by the Butterley company worked from 1830 to 1965 when it was replaced by an electric winder. An identical 1830s engine still survives in working order at Middleton Top further up the trail. At Sheep Pasture Top there was also a small engine shed, because the locomotive which worked the Sheep Pasture to Middleton Foot section was cut off from the rest of the railway system by two great inclines.

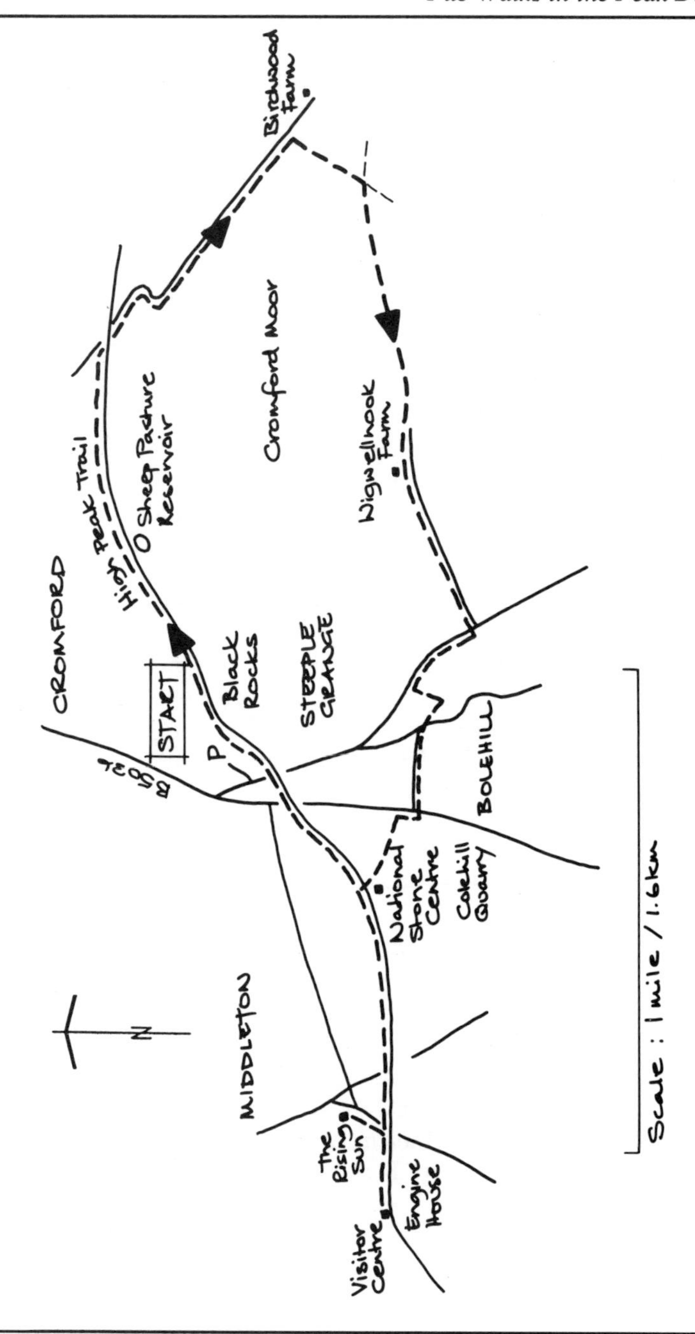
Birchwood Farm
High Peak Trail
Sheep Pasture Reservoir
Cromford Moor
Wigwellnook Farm
CROMFORD
START
P
B5036
Black Rocks
STEEPLE GRANGE
BOLEHILL
National Stone Centre
Colehill Quarry
MIDDLETON
N
The Rising Sun
Engine House
Visitor Centre
Scale : 1 mile / 1.6km

Begin the descent of Sheep Pasture incline. After a short descent the trail crosses over a bridge, before which there is a sign post to Alderwasley. Go right here and descend onto a rough lane leaving the trail behind. The lane pursues an easy course through beautiful deciduous woodland for a short way, then turns sharp right along the side of the wood, with trees to the right and fields to the left. A sharp left turn takes you away from the wood. The lane, sometimes quite wide now runs between fields. After almost half a mile at the corrugated-asbestos barn, go right, through a stile (easily missed) into fields.

The path is indistinct but keep the wall to your left through two fields. Then go through a stile in the left hand corner of the second field. Cross the top of another narrow field to a further stile where you go right along a tractor track. This enters another field and follows a course straight across the middle. Two fields are crossed this way then a narrow stile leads into yet another field where the path is indistinct, but the wall on the left is a sure guide. At the end of the field a cart track is picked up again and this is followed over the remnants of Cromford Moor to Wigwell Farm

The farm is skirted by the track which now becomes a tarmac lane. On reaching the main road, go right, crossing onto the pavement. Descend for a short way then, just after the left hand bend, there is a short row of cottages below you on the left. At the end of these there is a flight of steps, not signposted, which lead down past the end of the terrace. It descends quite steeply slanting first right then left to emerge onto The Lanes, a lovely backwater. This is part of Bolehill hamlet, an area well known for its subsidence. Go right and follow The Lanes down to another road. Go right again then, at the next junction, which has the delightful name of Nan Gells Hill, go left, down to the main Cromford to Wirksworth road.

National Stone Centre

At the main road, go right, across the road and at the bus stop take the path to the left. The start of the path from the main road is not signed and seems more like a private drive but be assured it is a public right of way which leads straight to the Visitor Centre of the National Stone Centre. This new venture examines the history and development of stone quarrying, its methods and how stone is used. The area is fascinating having been worked continuously for minerals, lead fluorspar and limestone since Saxon times, if not earlier. There are some fine examples of reef limestone but it is hard to envisage this as being a tropical lagoon at one time in pre-history!

The path goes under the High Peak Trail by a fine stone bridge. Do not go under the Trail but turn right just before the bridge, up a path leading to the Trail itself. At the trail go left along the embankment with a tremendous view over Wirksworth and down the Ecclesbourne valley. Coalhills quarry, part of The Stone Centre, is on the right. On the left, beyond the remains of a loading gauge, is the site of the former branch line which linked the High Peak and Wirksworth railways with a one in four gradient!

Middleton Top

A short distance further on, the trail widens at the foot of the Middleton incline – at one time an important railway centre on this very rural line. Climb the incline to Middleton Top to visit the well preserved engine house. Then descend the incline again (retracing your steps) and just before the first bridge go left through a stile and take the waymarked footpath which leads unerringly down to the Rising Sun.

Leaving the pub go down to the crossroads and turn right towards Wirksworth. Go under the bridge and turn left over the stile to regain the Trail again at the bottom of Middleton Incline. Retrace your steps along the Trail past the Stone Centre and along the Trail as it swings to the left. Ahead now can be seen the TV mast at Bole Hill. Below lies the Black Rocks car park. On the left is Steeplehouse Quarry, famed for the fossilised shark teeth found there in great numbers. A little further on was the dubiously named Killers Branch Railway which served the Middleton limestone mine. A group of enthusiasts has now re opened part of this as a narrow gauge line using mine engines and rolling stock. On the right the two houses formed Steeplehouse station. On one memorable occasion the locomotive fell off the embankment into the garden of the station house and great difficulty was experienced in getting it out again.

Continue now on the last lap of the walk crossing Steeple Arch Bridge over the B5036 road to return to Black Rocks again.

WALK 17: MILLER'S DALE

The Route: Monsal Trail, Blackwell Hall, Priestcliffe Ditch. A short walk but with several climbs.

Distance: 5 miles

Start: Miller's Dale old station. Map Reference: 138733

Map: Ordnance Survey Outdoor Leisure Map No 24 – The Peak District, White Peak Area.

How to get there:

By Bus – There is a daily service between Sheffield and Buxton calling at Miller's Dale.

By Car – Travel on the B6049 off the A6 or A623 road to Miller's Dale. Follow the signs to the car park at the old station.

The Angler's Rest at Miller's Dale is a basic pub only a short distance from the River Wye. There is a bar and a lounge and dining area. The landlord serves Tetley bitter and Burton ale on hand pull, and bar food. Its clientele is a mixture of locals, walkers and youth hostellers from the nearby Ravenstor hostel. It can get busy during the summer months as Miller's Dale attracts a large number of visitors especially on a Sunday.

There is a cafe in Miller's Dale opposite to the entrance to the old railway station for those who prefer a cup of tea or coffee. This is open most days for refreshment.

As you can see from the size of the station, Miller's Dale was an important community, being a junction for Buxton off the then main Manchester to Derby line. It was also, as the name suggests, an important local milling centre with Litton Mill further down the valley being significant.

The Walk

From the railway station, walk along the Monsal Trail away from the viaducts and station platforms to pass old water tanks and then lime kilns opened in the 1880s and evidently worked until 1944. The kilns may be inspected and interpretation material is provided on the site. Not far beyond, as you approach the bridge over the River Wye, go right, down to the river bank. Turn right and follow the narrow and often watery path through a delightful section of countryside until the valley widens and a footbridge comes into sight.

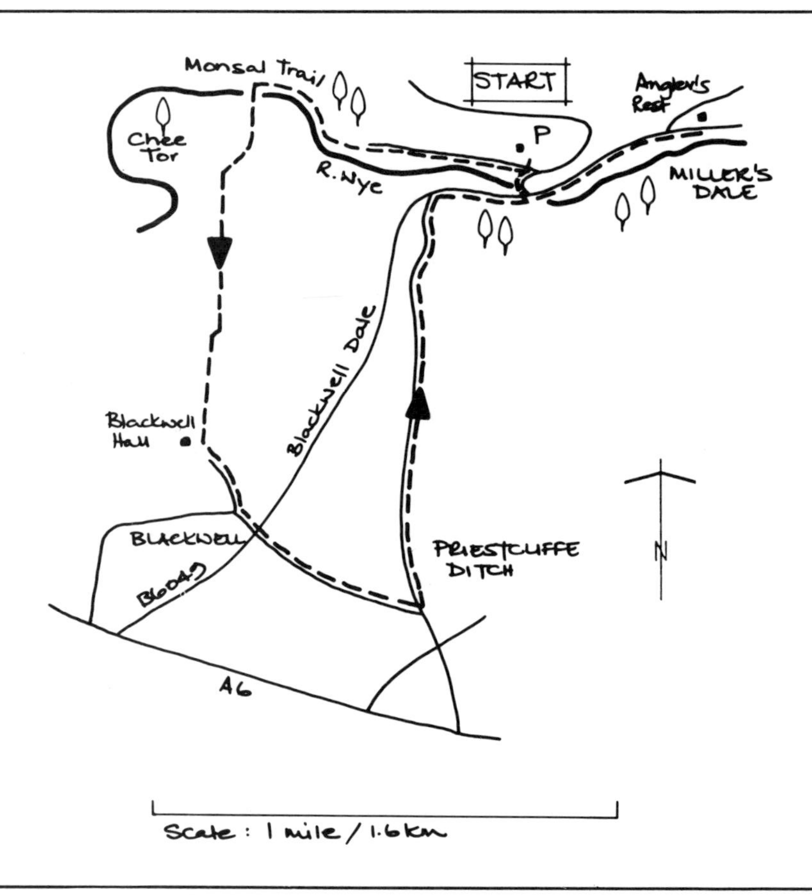

Chee Tor

Cross the bridge and then be careful not to walk along a clear path which climbs slightly right up the hill. Your way is less distinct on the ground. Go slightly left at first through an area of scrub then go right zig-zagging your way up a steep edge out of the dale. The ground levels as you pause awhile to admire the views across Chee Tor and up Chee Dale. Keep ahead to a wooden marker post and onto a signpost by a broken wall. Go ahead to join a dry stone wall and cross a stile in the wall, go right and then left along the wall. At the top of the field go over a stile by a gate and then go left along a track through an area cultivated as a nursery.

Blackwell Hall

The track passes farm buildings, curves left and proceeds through a spinney by Blackwell Hall. Walk down the tree lined drive which curves down to a road. Go left and shortly cross the main road. Keep ahead along a road which climbs up to Priestcliffe Ditch. As this road curves right beyond the houses, go left down a track which slowly but surely drops into Blackwell Dale.

It eventually exits onto the road leading into Miller's Dale. Cross the road and walk along the narrow grass verge for the short distance back into the village. If thirsty continue ahead after the bridge and take the next right for the pub. If returning to the old station, go left after the bridge and bear left at the corner to climb a path back up to the station. If Peak Rail succeed in their ambitions, this station will come back to life once more as part of an ambitious scheme to span the Peak District with a leisure railway. Steam hauled trains through the valley would seem most unusual after such a lapse in time.

WALK 18: MONSAL HEAD

Route: Top of Monsal Dale, Monsal Trail, Little Longstone. A gentle walk with no real climbs.

Distance: 5 miles

Start: Monsal Head Hotel. Map Reference: 185716

Map: Outdoor Leisure Series Map No 24 – The Peak District, White Peak Area

How to get there:

By Bus – There is a bus service from Bakewell and Tideswell on Mondays to Saturdays. There is also a limited Summer Sunday service.

By Car – Travel on the B6465 road between the main A623 road at Wardlow Mires and the A6 road at Ashford in the Water.

The Pack Horse is a fine little pub which has been sitting prettily in the hamlet of Little Longstone in very much the same way for the past two hundred years or so. The pub serves Marstons beers on hand pull and has two rooms both of which are used by walkers. The garden area is ideal for children and the Pack Horse is well known for its exceptional bar food.

The pub is open weekday lunchtimes as well as evenings so is ideal for the thirsty rambler.

If not stopping here, The Stables bar behind the Monsal Head Hotel also serves a good pint in congenial surroundings. The stalls are large and comfortable and ideal for family or small gatherings. The large fireplace and manger stand at the top of the room but without an open fire. The beers on sale are Theakstons, including the leg-buckling Old Peculiar so take it easy if you have a pot of this liquorice-like brew. The Stables bar is open all day so there is no need to worry if the ramble takes longer than expected. Food and coffee is also available.

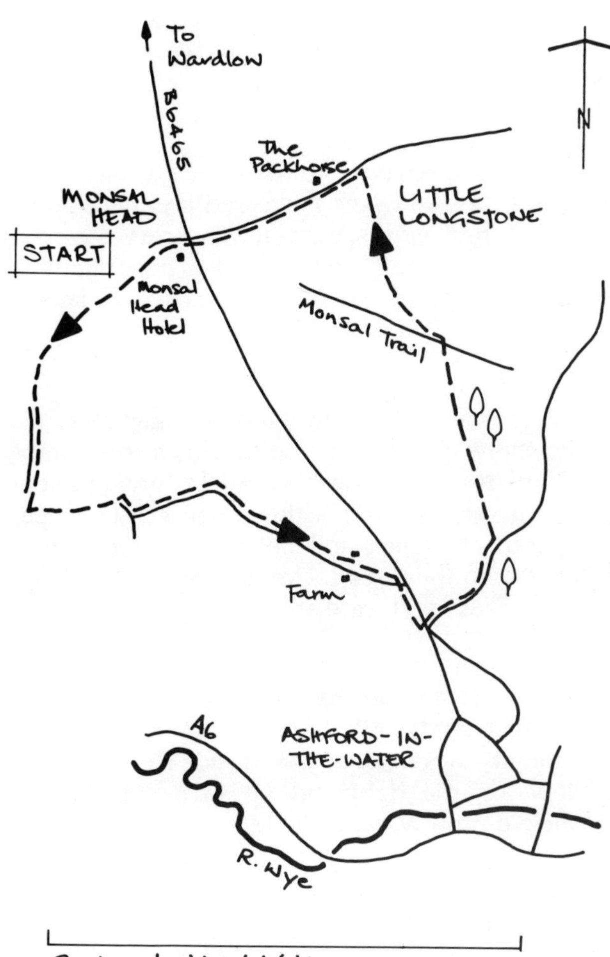
To Wardlow
B6465
N
The Packhorse
MONSAL HEAD
LITTLE LONGSTONE
START
Monsal Head Hotel
Monsal Trail
Farm
A6
ASHFORD-IN-THE-WATER
R. Wye
Scale : 1 mile / 1.6 km

The Walk

Start from the entrance to The Monsal Head Hotel. Turn left along the Cressbrook road which passes two cafes and The Stables bar. The road disappears down the side of the dale but you keep ahead through a gap stile to the wooded shoulder of the valley. The view is exceptional, over the viaduct and up the Wye valley.

Take the narrower high level path which climbs gently to the left. It leads through scrub to a stile which is crossed and then up to a wider green path along the top by a drystone wall. This curves gently to a stile which is crossed by a gate leading into a walled track. Continue ahead, soon to give out into a field, but continue straight on to another walled stretch which again brings you to a gap stile adjacent to what look like old church railings.

Walk to the field corner and then turn left over a gap stile. Walk down the field with a drystone wall to your right. This meets another walled lane which you follow for a short distance before turning left at the first junction. The track curves right and within a short distance passes farm buildings. Keep ahead as signed and not slightly right into the farm yard. The track exits onto the B road. Go right and walk along the road edge to the junction. Cross with care and turn left along the quiet back lane.

The lane passes a few houses and then bends to the right before a strip of woodland. Go left over the stile here to walk a well trodden route through a succession of stiles more or less ahead. The path climbs gently alongside the wood on the right and up to a stile just before the embankment of the old railway, now The Monsal Trail.

Cross the embankment and down the other side into another field. Go left down the field to cross a stile and then follow the worn path through a gap stile and onwards towards the buildings of Little Longstone, through parkland. Exit by way of the large stone stile by a gate and once on the road, turn left.

There is a pavement alongside the road to Monsal Head and as it is a climb all of the way, it might be judicious to call at the Pack Horse to gather your strength for the final stretch.

WALK 19: MONYASH

Route: Bagshaw Dale, Lathkill Dale, One Ash Grange Farm, Fern Dale. A well walked series of paths with generally easy walking.

Distance: 6 miles

Start: The Bulls Head, Village Green. Map Reference: 150666

Map: Ordnance Survey Outdoor Leisure Map No 24 – The Peak District, White Peak Area.

How to get there:

By Bus – There is a limited Mondays to Saturdays service to Monyash from Bakewell and Buxton.

By Car – Monyash is on the B5055 between the Ashbourne to Buxton road and Bakewell. There is a car park in the village near to the green.

The pub, which dates from the 17th century, has now reverted to its old name after a brief flirtation as The Hobbit. No prizes for guessing where that name of the pub came from. Tolkien might not be too happy to have pubs named after his mythical characters. Needless to say, it is popular with walkers and often at weekends you will come across dozens of pairs of boots sitting neatly outside the front door.

It is a basic pub with a long bar serving Marston's beers and bar food. Do take care if you choose the Pedigree for it is a strong brew to go walking on. In the summer, ramblers spill out onto the few seats outdoors to admire the traditional village green with cross and memorial while supping away. In the author's experience this pub tends to be closed on weekday lunchtimes but is definitely open at weekends and evenings.

Monyash is deceiving for it looks as if it has been engaged in agriculture for its entire existence. This is only partly true, for in earlier times it was the centre of local mining, so much so that it had a Barmote court as in Wirksworth. The area is known for its small meres formed on beds of clay and served by limestone springs. One of these still exists near to the green and is enclosed by a wall, presumably built at one time to keep out animals. The church spire is often reflected in the mere's calm waters, a delightful building much restored through the ages.

Walkers outside The Hobbit, (now The Bulls Head) Monyash (courtesy of Chris Rushton, Evening Sentinel)

The Walk

Start from the entrance to The Bulls Head on the village green. At one time this was the site of a local market dating from a charter granted in 1340. A fair is still held here twice a year. Turn right and right again to pass by the car park, at one time a pool with a well for public use. Walk by the methodist chapel dating from 1888 although a century earlier there was a very strong Quaker community here. Walk along the street to the end of the village. Turn right at the junction for Sheldon and then go right again beneath a tree and through two gap stiles in close succession. This is Bagshaw Dale and the path is clearly defined, crossing two more stiles before reaching the B road.

Ricklow Quarry

Cross over the main road and continue down the dale to a stile which leads into a deeper boulder filled section, passing by the old Ricklow Quarry on the left. Nearby is Parsons Tor, so named because a local vicar in Monyash plunged to his death here in 1776. The path enters a nature reserve and continues alongside a drystone wall and fence down

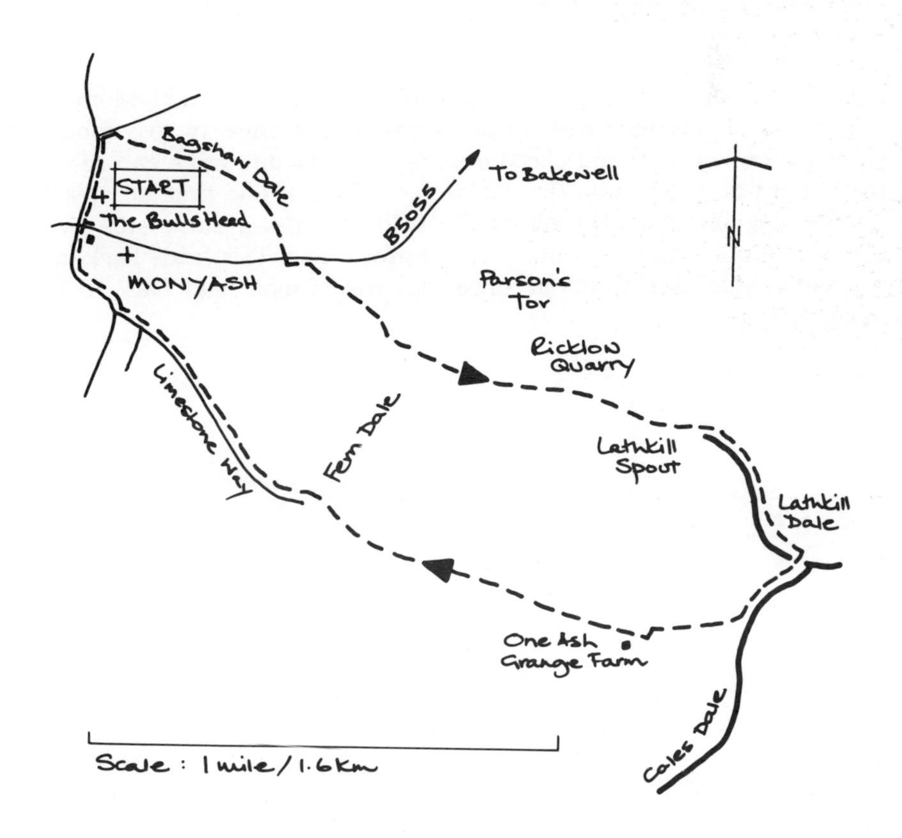

the valley into Lathkill Dale. On the right you will notice Lathkill Head Cave, the source of the River Lathkill, mainly dry in summer but in winter it gushes forth and runs down the field bottom with a vengeance.

Cales Dale

At the footbridge your way is to the right over it into Cales Dale. The well worn path leads up the valley, narrowing as it climbs up to the right beneath a limestone wall and out of the dale by way of a stile into a wide green gap. Walk ahead to the farm and head for the steps between barns. The track passes by the old One Ash Grange Farm, curving left and then right away from the farmhouse. This track gives out through a gateway at the top of the field into another very large field. Go left here and keep company with the wall on the left.

In the corner of the field go left over a stile and then turn right. Monyash village comes into sight. Keep ahead towards the village to cross another stile by a broken wall and ahead once again to go through a gap stile at the bottom of a field into the top of Fern Dale, at one time an area of mining. Go slightly right across the field to cross a stone stile by a signpost. Go left and left into a walled green lane. This leads back into back into Monyash. Continue ahead on the tarmac road back to the village green.

WALK 20: PARWICH

The Route: Cobblersnook Plantation, Roystone Grange, Two Dale Barn, Parwich Close Farm, Foufinside, Middlemoor, Uppermoor. A walk in a quieter part of The Peak District.

Distance: 7 miles

Start: Minninglow Car Park. Map Reference: 194582

Map: Ordnance Survey Outdoor Leisure Map No 24 – The Peak District, White Peak Area.

How to get there:

By Bus – There is a bus service on Summer Sundays only to Pikehall from Buxton, Glossop and Huddersfield. Parwich has an infrequent service to Ashbourne.

By Car – Minninglow Car Park is signed off the A5012 Cromford to Newhaven road.

The Sycamore is a smashing little village local with three pleasant rooms, often with open fires burning in the winter months to warm the feet. The publicans, Don and Lynda Keyworth, offer handpulled Bass and serve food at lunchtimes and early evenings. The pub opens on weekday lunchtimes between 1130 and noon and closes around 2.30pm depending on trade. It reopens at 7 pm in the evening.

Walkers are welcome at The Sycamore but you are reminded to treat the inn as you would your own front room, i.e. avoid muddy boots and the like. There are, as one would expect in this area, trophies hanging in the bar from Shrovetide football games played in Ashbourne and brought back by burly regulars who partake in this famous annual pastime.

The Walk

Leave Minninglow car park and turn right along the lane to the T-junction. Here, turn left alongside Cobblersnook Plantation. At the cross roads go left into Minninglow Lane. Note the remains of the old wooden signpost on the right, now sadly minus all of its arms. Minninglow Lane forms part of an ancient packhorse way running from Hartington to Wirksworth. The tree-crowned top of Minninglow is clearly in view from the lane, but the hill is not climbed on this walk.

Low

The word 'low', as explained in the introductory chapter, means hill and in Derbyshire the lows were very often used as burial places and were places of superstition and religious veneration. Frequently, they were crowned with trees and served as markers on cross country routes such as this. Another prominent feature ahead is one of the drystone embankments of the Cromford and High Peak Railway.

Where the tarmac gives out, go right, through a gateway and down a track to Roystone Grange. The track passes Roystone Cottages on the right and winds its way down the dry limestone dale. This is part of the Roystone Grange trail, for here is one of the most important archaeological sites in the Peak District. There is a continuous history of farming and occupation on this site going back before Roman times. Remains of various periods are still visible to the trained eye.

Roystone Rocks

As the farm buildings of Roystone Grange are reached, note on your left the curious curved roof 'barn' on the hillside. It was probably an explosives store for a nearby quarry. On the right the limestone thrusts through the soil appearing in weird weathered shapes. Once through the farmyard, the track forks. The main track goes left, down to the church like building and into a deeper dale. Your path bears right, climbing up the hillside with Roystone Rocks on the right and Roystone Plantation to your left. The track soon deteriorates to little more than a path and curves close to a wall on the left. Do not go through a gateway in this wall, but keep the wall to your left and go through the right hand

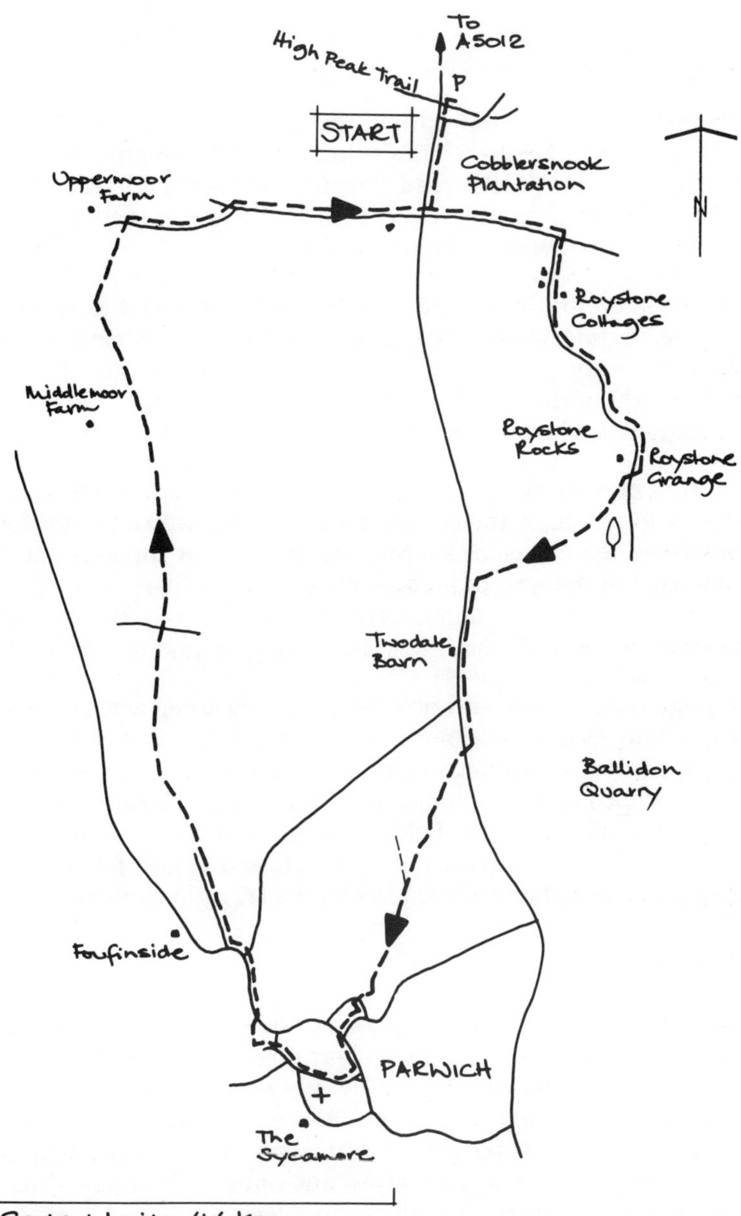
To A5012
High Peak Trail
P
START
Cobblersnook Plantation
N
Uppermoor Farm
Roystone Cottages
Middlemoor Farm
Roystone Rocks
Roystone Grange
Twodale Barn
Ballidon Quarry
Foufinside
PARWICH
The Sycamore
Scale : 1 mile/1.6 km

gateway in the cross wall ahead. The way forward is now more obvious, the gateway being marked by concrete gateposts.

Descend to join a road and go left. Shortly, just by the well-built Two Dale Barn, the road begins to climb out of the dale bottom and a fine dry valley diverges left. At the road junction bear left and ascend a steep little rise. The trees on the left are part of a screen belt for Ballidon Quarry, the edge of which can just be seen.

At the brow of the hill, there is a footpath sign on the right and a gateway leads into open fields. The path is none too clear along this section so be wary not to go astray. From the gateway go left to a gate just to the right of the hawthorn in the lower wall of the field. The Trent power stations are in view, as are the hills of Cannock Chase.

The path continues along the same alignment, crossing the next field diagonally to a stile in the corner. However, the walked path does not correspond to the ordnance survey map here, for it continues along the left hand side of the wall to a gateway beyond a solitary tree. There may have been a pond or building here at some time as there is an odd circular depression with the field wall curving around it.

Go through the gateway and now bear right, heading across the field to a stile roughly half way along the far wall. There is a very extensive view south from this vantage point. The alignment continues across the next field. Imperceptibly, another path joins from the right and the two converge at a stile. The next field is narrow and rough with hummocks and hollows. The path is obvious though and heads for a stile by a dew-pond and solitary hawthorn tree in the far right corner.

Parwich

The village of Parwich is now in view. At the wall corner, bear left down the hill, the path being signed by a short post with a yellow waymarker. The path enters an area of scrub and twists and turns its way down. The path steepens and there is one particularly rocky and sometimes slippery section so care has to be taken. You soon reach the first houses of Parwich, however and a stile gives out onto a driveway. This soon becomes a narrow lane passing the former Parwich Hospital on the right and descending to a road junction.

Fork left here and continue down the hill towards the church. The road levels and passes a more recent housing development on the right. At the next junction go right, past the church along to the village green and 'main' road. The Sycamore public house, is just down the road to the left. On leaving the pub, retrace your steps to pass the duck pond and at the village green bear left along the road signed to Alsop and Newhaven. At the next junction go straight on, signed to Newhaven and Buxton, bearing left by the shop, then right past the school.

This appears to be a dead end but a path continues to the right at the back of the cottages to emerge on the road again. Go left here and prepare to leave Parwich behind. Note Rose Cottage with its cave on the right. The vicarage is on the left and then at the next junction keep left (signed Newhaven). The road bends sharply to the left and at this point there is a stile and signpost on the right. Go through the stile into the field and ascend to the wall ahead. Follow the wall around to the right, to a gateway in the corner of the field. Go through the gateway, then turn immediately right into a narrow and sometimes muddy green lane partly overgrown with scrub. The left hand boundary soon becomes a line of scattered bushes and a stile near a trough carries the path into open fields. Keep alongside the wall on your right to a gateway in the corner. Here, go right then immediately left across a muddy patch into a field which shows signs of mediaeval ridge and furrow farming practice.

Rocky Knoll

The path keeps alongside the wall on the left, surmounts a little rocky knoll, then goes through a stile at the left hand end of the little clump of trees. The path turns right to a stile, well hidden between two sycamore trees before continuing its steady upward course with the wall still on the left. At the end of the long narrow field, the path passes through a gateway and the next stile can be seen silhouetted on the skyline, to the right of a lone tree. Keep your eye on the tree because the stile disappears from view again and there is no obvious path on the ground. The view from the top of this field is extensive so pause a while to catch your breath.

Go through the stile and cross the broad green lane before going through a gateway straight ahead. The next stile is to the right of the gap in the far wall. Again, there is no obvious path but the route goes up the middle of the field bearing slightly right. In the next field there is confusion. The ordnance survey map indicates that you should walk alongside a boundary wall but this has now gone. The best practical option is to walk straight across the middle of this field, more or less on the same alignment as you were on previously.

At the far side of the field, roughly in the middle of the wall, there is a stile to the right of the concrete trough. Go over this stile, then turn left to walk alongside the wall, through another field to a shelter belt of trees. Do not, follow the broad track to the right which leads to a gateway, but go through a stile in the wall ahead. Minninglow is now in view to the right beyond Roystone Rocks.

Your path now crosses another line of trees, not shown on the map, and then through another stile into open fields again. Middlemoor Farm lies just to your left. Once in this next field keep straight ahead parallelling the boundary wall of the wood on your right and thus locating a stile in the far wall. In the next field there should be a stile in the wall almost in line with the building on the skyline, but there is nothing obvious except a few pieces of wood. Therefore, go through the gateway in the left hand corner of the field. The next stile lies just to the right of the far left corner of the field, again in line with Uppermoor Farm and marked by a thorn tree. This takes you into a rough field. Ignoring the gateway to the right, head across to the nearest thorn tree where there is a stile in the wall. This leads into another rough field where there has once been a building.

Uppermoor

The path skirts around the end of this field but does not go through the gateway on the right, prefering instead to use a stile to the right of the thorn tree. The final ascent now begins to Uppermoor Farm, with a wall and thorns on the right and views over to the gritsone moors beyond Sheen on the left.

As Uppermoor Farm is approached, a pronounced track is encountered running across your line of walk. Join it, to go through a gateway on the right along the south side of Uppermoor Plantation. This is not shown as a footpath on the map as it is actually a public road! The chances of meeting anything motorised, however, is very remote. Continue alongside the wood and with Minninglow in clear view ahead begin the last stretch to the starting point.

Keep the wall on your left through three fields before entering a narrow walled lane. This is soon joined by another green lane known as Cobblersnook Lane and together they lead steadily down towards a prominent white house known as The Nook. Just beyond The Nook at a cross roads, go left and retrace your steps to Minninglow car park.

WALK 21: ROWSLEY

The Route: Caudwells Mill, Rowsley Moor Wood, Calton Pastures, Calton Lees, Bank Wood End. From Rutland to Devonshire and back without leaving Derbyshire!

Distance: 4 Miles

Start: Caudwells Mill Car Park. Map Reference: 255658. Alternatively use Calton Lees Car Park in Chatsworth Park.

Map: Ordnance Survey Outdoor Leisure Map No 24 – The Peak District, White Peak Area.

How to get there:

By Bus – There are a daily bus services from Manchester, Nottingham and Derby, Buxton, Bakewell and Matlock.

By Car – Travel on the A6 to Rowsley then follow the signs to Caudwell's Mill car park. For Calton Lees Car Park follow the signs for Chatsworth. The Car Park is signed within the Park.

The Grouse and Claret at first sight seems a reasonable pub name, offering a combination of rich food and drink. However, the inn sign shows a brightly coloured fish hook! The explanation is that both the Wye and Derwent are renowned trout rivers and 'grouse and claret' is the name given to one of the fly fishing hook designs.

The old name for the pub was the Railway, being not far from Rowsley railway station. The pub serves hand-pulled Mansfield beers and provides an array of lunchtime and evening bar meals. There are three rooms, a public bar, lounge and games room. Outside there is a seating area with tables and these are very popular with families and walkers in the summer. The pub has recently been renovated and is now much more geared to serving food. Nevertheless, walkers are still welcome.

The Walk

From Caudwell's Mill car park follow the footpath into the mill complex. The mill was rescued from complete closure, dereliction and demolition by dint of hard work and cash. It is now run by a trust and makes a superb visit either before or after the ramble. There is also a pottery, glass blowing, and a well-stocked craft shop and picture gallery. There is also a restaurant. The car park can be very busy hence the alternative of Calton Lees. Whichever you use, make sure you visit the mill.

Haddon Hall

Pass the craft shop and go through the mill yard to the A6, where the stops are for those coming by bus. Cross the road and head up Church Lane by the well site on the left and The Peacock Hotel on the right. Rowsley was, and to some extent still is, an estate village belonging to the Dukes of Rutland, who retain a strong influence on the landholding in this area. The ducal seat is Haddon Hall, a superb example of an Elizabethan manor house, just up the A6 road towards Bakewell.

Go up Church Lane, passing the site of the railway bridge and entrance to St Katherine's church. Near the last houses in Rowsley there is a stone trough and a seat on the left with fine views down the valley to Matlock. The tarmac lane deteriorates into a track which can become muddy after rain. When the trees are reached the track turns sharp right and climbs steeply. The track splits three ways and is barred by two metal gates. Take the left path which is waymarked as a bridleway. It leads through mixed woodland and begins to rise gently until three large beech trees are reached. The track passes between the second and third (left to right) and then forks. Your way is to the right, following the edge of the wood with the wall to the left. In a short distance the track leaves the wall and for plunges into the wood. At the crossing of paths go left along a well used path and follow the gently rising track with larch woods to the left and the mixed beech wood to the right.

Boundary

Another path joins from the left but keep straight on until a T junction is reached. The main track continues ahead but the path you are following

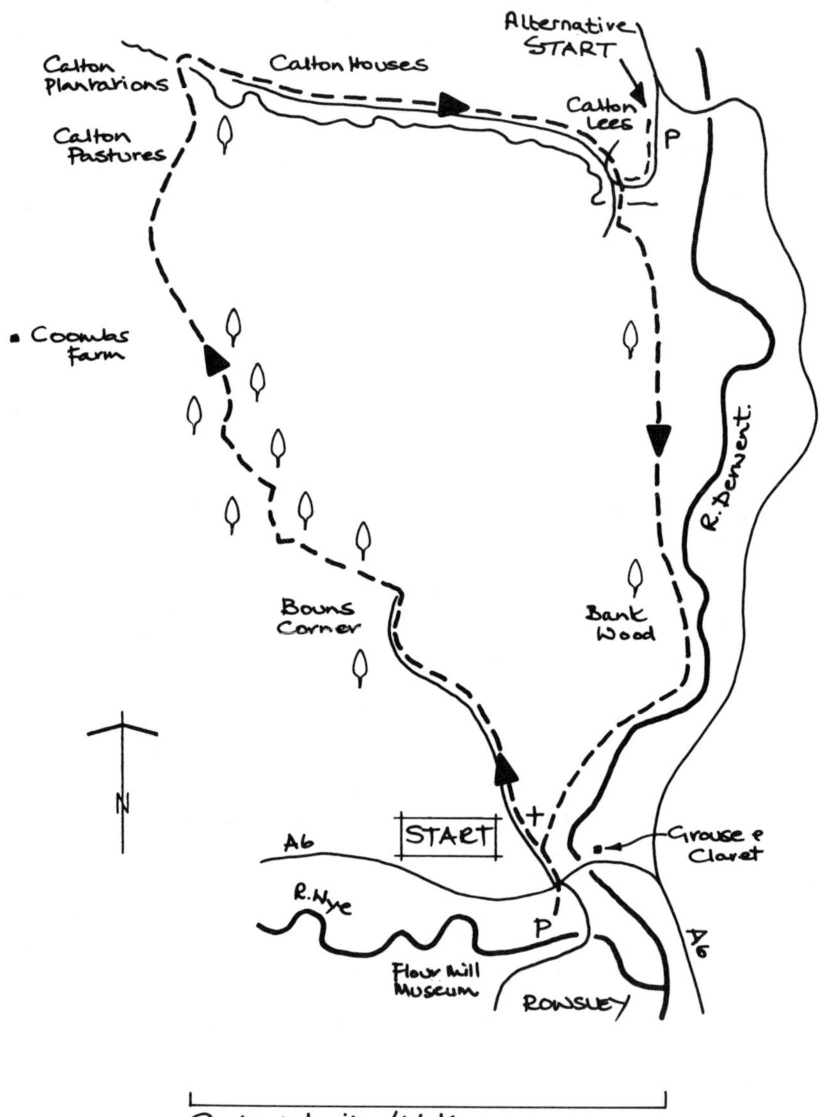
Alternative
START
Calton Plantations
Calton Houses
Calton Lees
P
Calton Pastures
Coombs Farm
R. Derwent
Bouns Corner
Bank Wood
N
START
A6
Grouse & Claret
R. Wye
P
A6
Flour Mill Museum
ROWSLEY
Scale : 1 mile / 1.6 Km

leads right, signed with a blue bridleway mark. The path climbs steadily upward, being somewhat slippery when wet until it is finally deflected leftwards by a large stone wall. This wall marks the boundary of the Haddon and Chatsworth estates in the ownership of the Dukes of Rutland and Devonshire respectively.

The gradient now eases and the path runs alongside the wall on the Rutland side with thick woodland to the left and right until an open area is reached which gives a glimpse downward towards Coombs Farm and Bakewell. Here there is a gateway in the wall and the path crosses into Devonshire land. The Ordnance survey map implies that the path continues on the Rutland side a little further, but there is no evidence of it on the ground as most walkers use the gateway and track which is the signed route.

Beyond the gateway the track swings away left and soon comes into a forest ride through which strides a power line. The track winds its way along the ride until a gate is reached. Once again, the ordnance survey map suggests that the bridleway continues through this gate but Chatsworth Estates have signed the path through a gap in the wall to the right then alongside another wall to a step stile.

Calton Houses

Here you come out of the trees and are greeted with a panorama of Chatsworth Park. The Russian cottage can be seen on the hillslope opposite and down the valley lies Calton Houses. Once over the stile follow the blue bridleway mark, not the yellow footpath marker. Head off across the turf using the clump of trees in the valley bottom as a marker. There is no obvious path on the ground but once over the brow of the hill there is another blue waymark.

A path now materialises and crosses a slight dip just below the troughs to come to a broad hollow way. The track runs alongside the trees turning sharp right to cross the Calton Lees Brook as a culvert. Once over, there is a gate and a stile and, just beyond, a blue waymark. Your route goes to the right alongside the wood until a gateway is reached on the right. Again, there are blue waymarks and this time go right, through the gate and into a narrow walled lane. This leads down through the picturesque hamlet of Calton Houses and once clear of the last house, descends by means of a zig-zag to come alongside the brook.

The way is now clear ahead, a rough surfaced lane leading gently down the hill with the brook always to the right. Ignore tracks to the left and right but keep on downstream in a beautifully quiet part of Chatsworth Park. After roughly three-quarters of a mile, the track curves through a gateway and reaches a cross roads at Calton Lees. (If you are parked at Calton Lees car park go straight on here, past the garden centre and so reach your car. Take the right turn and cross the brook. If you are starting from Calton Lees car park walk on the lane past the garden centre until the hamlet is reached then go left at the cross roads. Go up through the little village, one of several Chatsworth estate villages. Just past the last house, the road bears right and there is a footpath sign to a stile on the left. This takes you into the fields for the last stretch of the ramble to Rowsley.

Derwent

Keep left alongside the wall with a fine view over the Derwent to the village of Beeley. In a short distance, a step stile on the left takes you over a wall and the path then goes right, following the wall until it strikes off across the field to a gateway in the fence. Beyond this a well marked path runs across the meadows through a series of fields until it approaches the Derwent. The name Derwent derives from the Celtic *Dwrwen* which translates as 'the river by the oakwoods'. Now, the oaks look thin on the ground but there are plenty of alders to compensate. On the other hand, the Welsh word 'wern' refers to alders, so that might be an explanation.

The path leads to a stile in a wall on the right. You are now back in Rutland and a narrow slippery path leads through scrub and into open fields again. Follow the wall, but where it turns right and there is a track leading away from the river, go straight on, keeping company with the river to a gateway and stile. The path here is difficult with trenches and muddy pools in places. It descends to pass under the railway arch and past a farmyard before mercifully disgorging onto the road. Turn left along the village street, and at The Peacock turn left along the A6 to go over the Derwent by a fine bridge. Originally this was a packhorse bridge but has been much widened over the centuries. This leads to the Grouse and Claret. Return over the bridge and follow the signs back to Caudwell's Mill.

WALK 22: STARKHOLMES

The Route: Starkholmes, Riber, Hearthstone, Bilberry Knoll, Coombs Wood, Castletop, Wood End and Woodseats

Distance: 3 miles

Start: The White Lion, Starkholmes. Map Reference: 301588

Map: Ordnance Survey Leisure Map No 24 – The Peak District, White Peak Area.

How to get there:

By Bus or train: On Mondays to Saturdays there is a bus from Matlock and Cromford. There is a daily bus and train service to Matlock Bath with a half mile walk up Bath Fields to the White Lion.

By Car – From the A6 south, turn right at Cromford crossroads, go over the bridge and turn left. From the A6 north, travel to Matlock and then on the A615 to Matlock Green, where you turn right to Starkholmes. Roadside parking is available, but please park tidyly.

The White Lion is a Home Ales pub which also provides food and offers a superb view over Matlock Bath on a sunny day. The publicans, Mike and Esme Page, serve a delicious pint of Home Ales and Theakstons XB from handpulls. Meals are served at lunchtimes and the pub is open from 1145 am until 3 pm, reopening again at 6.30 pm in the evening. In the summer, opening is earlier at 6 pm and early evening meals are offered.

There is a good local trade at this inn, but visitors are made most welcome. The beer garden is ideal for families and thus is often well used. This is deservedly a firm favourite for the walker who enjoys a good pint to refresh the parts which constantly need refreshing.

The Gardens, Matlock

The Walk

Leaving the pub, go right towards Matlock along the road. Take care as there is no footpath. Where the road is separated from the houses on the left by iron railings, look out for a flight of steps on the opposite side and go up these to emerge on another road at a hairpin bend. Follow the road up the hill and where it enters another right hand hairpin bend, go straight on along a signed footpath.

This starts as a narrow lane, the continues as a metalled path down the left hand side of Falconcliffe House. The route looks like a private path to someone's back garden, especially as there is a garden gate across it at the end of the house. Nonetheless, it is the public path, so go through the gate and the garden over a stile and into fields. Surprisingly, the field path is still tarmac and a short branch leads off right to a spring and trough, probably a local water supply until the mains water was laid on. The main path continues distinctly through a few more fields then just beyond a row of pine trees there is a crossing of paths.

Riber Castle

Go right here, ascending quite steeply towards Riber Castle which can be seen on top of the hill. The path is paved as it continues up hill crossing a farm drive. Beyond this point the path is confined by a wall on the left and a hedge on the right. It soon emerges into a field again, only to become coralled once again as the top of the hill is reached. The path skirts the northern boundary of Riber Castle and soon comes to the main entrance.

Riber Castle is a Victorian construction, originally built in the 1860s as the home of John Smedley, who made his fortune out of Matlock hydros. As a house, it was not a success, nor was it satisfactory as a school. The building fell into ruin and was taken over as a zoo and wildlife sanctuary which it still is. Ambitious plans to turn it into an hotel seem to have foundered.

Follow the access road past the squat little battlement tower, noting with some amusement the air vent in the pseudo mediaeval wall. At the Y junction keep right but note the magnificent Jacobean mansion to the

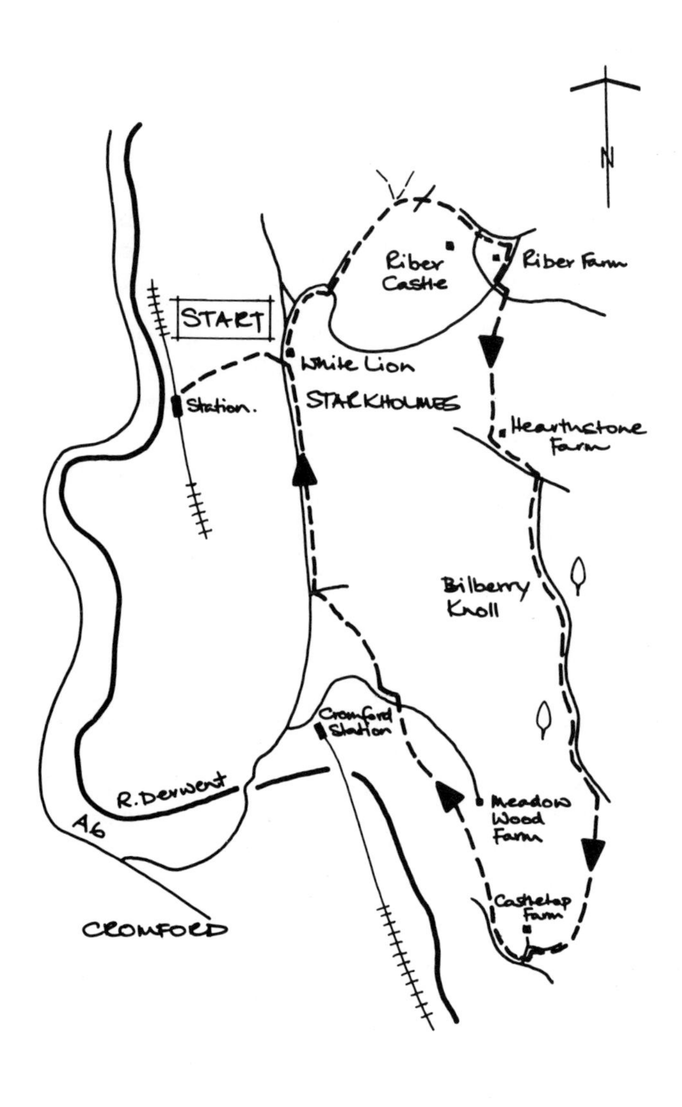
N
Riber Castle
Riber Farm
START
White Lion
Station.
STARKHOLMES
Hearthstone Farm
Bilberry Knoll
Cromford Station
R. Derwent
Meadow Wood Farm
A6
Castletop Farm
CROMFORD
Scale : 1 mile / 1.6 km.

left. Riber is blessed with some very fine old buildings. The next is Riber Farm which is also Jacobean and has a shop and tea rooms. Beyond is Riber Hall, now a high class restaurant.

At the triangle of roads, go left then almost immediately right through a gap stile by a telephone pole. Head across the field towards Hearthstone to a stile just to the right of an oak tree. Once in the next field, keep the wall or hedge on your right and carry on towards the farm buildings. There has been a fair amount of wall clearance here as the remains of the stiles testify and the land seems to be given over to the grazing of horses.

Hearthstone

At the boundary wall of the farm, keep right and head toward the gate, alongside which is a stile. Go through the stile into the lane and then go left through the hamlet of Hearthstone. Once clear of the buildings, continue along the lane until it forks. Take the right fork along a green lane bounded by gritstone walls.

Bilberry Knoll

The lane ascends gently and forks by a small plantation. Keep left here. This is Bilberry Knoll, the highest point of the walk. Once clear of the plantation there is a fine open aspect. The lane begins to descend and bends to the right. An overgrown track joins on the right and shortly afterwards the lane widens and then narrows, passing two stiles. Continue downwards with woodland to the right and fields to the left.

Once again, the lane forks and here keep right to drop to a gateway leading into open fields. The lane, if it can still be called this, heads across the field on an obvious terrace and there are excellent views over the Derwent to Cromford. The route continues across three fields in this manner. The house to the right is known as Castletop Farm but there is no known evidence of a castle here.

The track reaches a gate and stile where it becomes a walled lane again, bending right and then left at the farm access, then sharp right again at another access. At this point, the lane becomes a tarmac road descending past a beech wood. Just past this, beyond the electricty pole, go right at a stile and leave the lane.

Head across the field towards another electricity pole, keeping to the left of it as the field boundary is reached to pass through a well-hidden squeeze stile, not through the gap near the pole.

The stile gives out onto a tumbled landscape, almost certainly the result of landslips. The narrow path passes in front of a trough and spring. Go through the stile by the telegraph pole and follow the hedge and wall around towards the wood which now appears ahead. The wall bends left just after the gateway and is accompanied by a broad green track. Do not follow this but go straight ahead toward the wood where the timber work of the stile top can be seen. Go over the stile into the wood where the path is easily followed to emerge into open fields again at a stile.

The White Lion, Starkholmes

Solitary Stile

Head for a solitary stile between two electricity poles and join a farm track coming down from Meadow Wood Farm. Go along the farm track as it descends towards Cromford. The lane passes through a gateway and begins to bear left towards another gateway. However, a stile on the right gives out into fields this is your route. There is no obvious path until, breasting a small rise, you sight the two stones of a gap stile in the middle of the field. Head for these and a narrow path materialises.

Follow the narrow path past the stones, to a stile at the entrance to another wood. The path can get muddy here and fallen trees have to be circuited. Emerging from the wood head towards the green shed, noting left three new ponds. In the field corner by the shed go through a stile and shortly right onto a driveway to meet a road. Go right at the road. There is no footway but there is a verge of sorts on the left. Pass by the old school site and the war memorial to return to The White Lion.

Railway Station (Peak Rail), Matlock

WALK 23: TADDINGTON

The Route: Over Wheal, Deep Dale, Taddington Field. An easy walk to the isolated Deep Dale.

Distance: 6 miles

Start: The Queen's Arms. Map Reference: 144711

Map: Ordnance Survey Outdoor Leisure Map No 24 – The Peak District, White Peak Area.

How to get there:

By Bus – Taddington has a daily bus service between Nottingham, Derby and Manchester.

By Car – The village is signed off the A6 road. There is limited on street car parking in the village. Alternatively use the Peak Park's White Lodge Car Park on the A6 (shown on the map as P).

The Queen's Arms has been a popular calling point for ramblers over the years. It used to belong to Bass Charrington but is now a free house. It sells Mansfield beers in two bar areas, one a smaller bar by the side entrance, the other being the main L shaped lounge which is bedecked with brass. Be sure not to sit under the brass eagle which looks as if it is set to plummet from its perch at any moment.

There is a large attractive fireplace in the main room and also a piano for those with the urge to play. Food is served in the lounge and there is a limited seating area outside when the weather is fine.

Taddington could well be described as a linear sprawl with delightful roadside cottages saved nowadays from the thunder of quarry wagons which use the by pass. The mediaeval church is considerably larger than one would expect for a village of this size, a reflection of Taddington's former prosperity as a wool trading area. It was settled by inhabitants well before these times and there are several prehistoric mounds in the area, the most dramatic being Five Wells Tumulus on the moor between Taddington and Chelmorton.

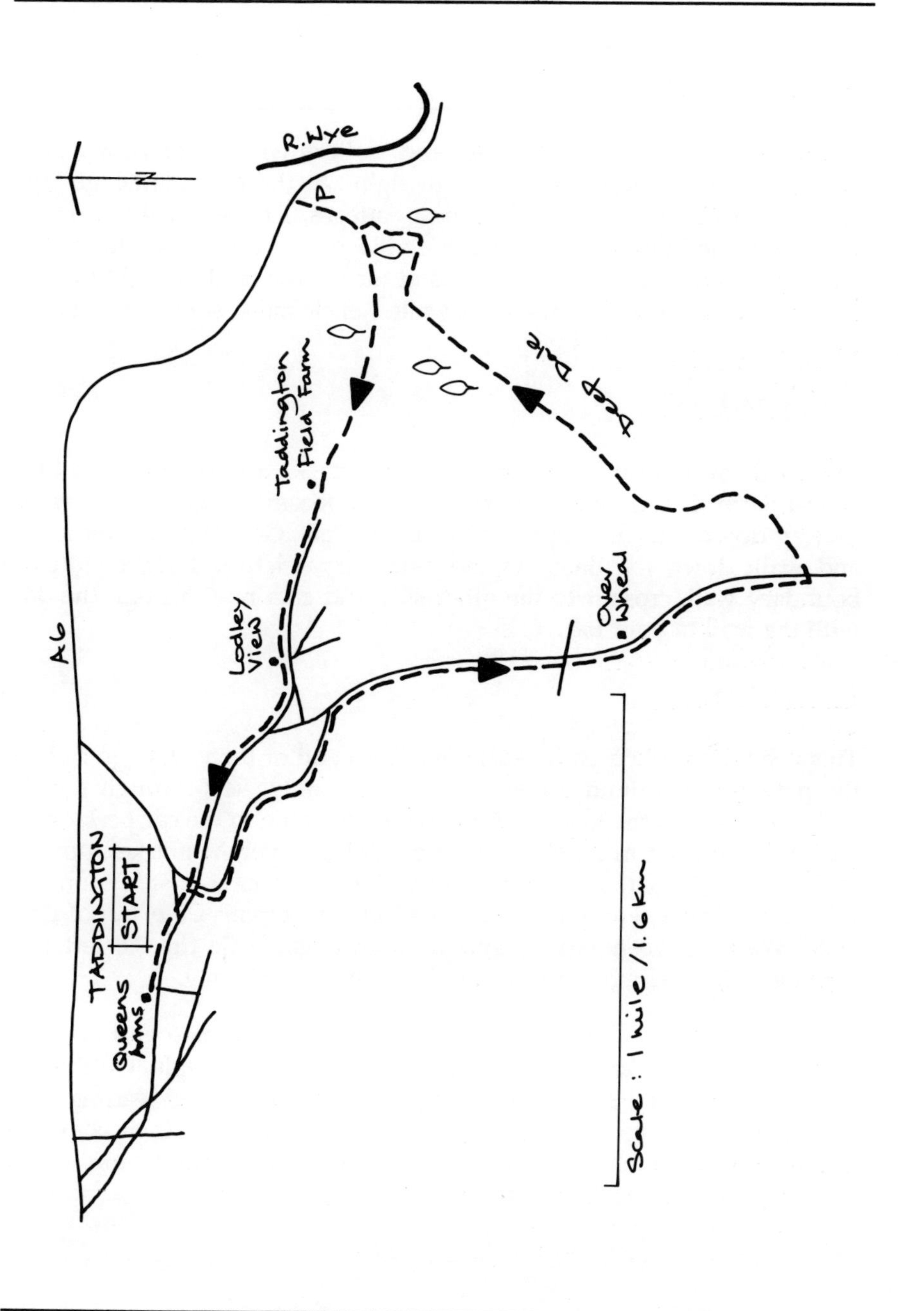
R. Wye
N
P
A6
Taddington Field Farm
Deep Dale
Lodley View
Over Wheal
TADDINGTON
START
Queens Arms
Scale : 1 mile / 1.6 Km

The Walk

From The Queen's Head turn left and walk down the road for a short distance to a junction where you go right. At the next corner go right again up a narrow track leading past cottages. At the junction turn left and climb the hillside away from the village. The track leads to another junction where you go left again and at the tarmac road go right to climb gently through a sea of drystone walled enclosures, some disturbed in the past by surface mining.

Over Wheal

The road levels near a junction of minor tracks and descends to Over Wheal Farm. Continue ahead and the track becomes rougher as it winds its way down into the upper end of Deep Dale. Go left here over a stile and walk down the dale. As the path curves left and right with the boundary wall, cross it to the other side and continue through the dale with the wall to your left.

Deep Dale

This is a well walked path. At the northern end of the valley, go right as the path bends around a crag and then cut down left through the dry valley and across the field as if you were returning to the car park on the A6. However, at a mid field point, signified by a yellow marker, turn left and walk up the bank through scrub and rocks to cross a stile. Continue up the dry valley, known as Dimmins Dale or Demons Dale, out of Deep Dale. Walk between bushes and through a gap stile on the left then turning right to climb in the same direction as previously.

The path leads up through woodland to a stile by a gate and ahead to Taddington Field Farm. Go over the step stile and turn right. Go through stiles to the left of a shed and left afterwards to join a road leading away from the farm. This climbs up to pass Lodley View and then continues down to a junction. Just before the junction cut off right onto a little track which soon meets the tarmac road again.

Follow the road back into Taddington.

WALK 24: THORPE

The Route: Spend Lane, Pike House, Hollington End, Tissington, Tissington Trail and Thorpe Cloud Station.

Distance: 4 miles

Start: Narlows Car Park. Map Reference: 164505

Map: Ordnance Survey Leisure Map No 24 – The Peak District, White Peak Area

How to get there:

By Bus – There is a limited bus service from Ashbourne, including Sundays.

By Car – Travel on the A515 between Ashbourne and Buxton. Thorpe is signed from this road at Tissington Gates. Narlows Car Park is on the right just before the Dog and Partridge road junction.

The Dog and Partridge is outside Thorpe village, standing at a crossroads of what used to be two important turnpike routes. The east to west route was part of a road from The Potteries to Bakewell. The potters required 'chert' from Bakewell for use in their glazing processes. The north to south route was part of the Buxton to Ashbourne road. Thus this coaching inn, with stables, has been host to travellers on foot and horseback for centuries.

There are several rooms, but in many respects the bar is most interesting for it includes a display of farm kitchen utensils. Your hosts Jacqui, Barbara, Eric Smith and Jim Taylor offer a rather tasty pint of Home bitter and provide an extensive menu for those seeking food. The pub is open from 1130 am until 3 pm in the summer and at 6.30 pm again in the evening. In the winter, lunch is usually from noon until 2 pm with a 7 pm opening. There's an outdoor area with a covered aviary to add interest.

The Walk

Leave the car park by the stile near to The Dog and Partridge and turn right to begin the climb of Spend Lane. The importance of this lane is obvious from a glance at the width between boundary walls. Turnpikes usually had a wall to wall width of forty feet and this is no exception. Fortunately the tarmac is now single track and cars are seldom seen.

As the lane nears Pike House on the left, there is a fine view of Thorpe Cloud, the miniature mountain guarding the entrance to Dovedale. At the National Trust sign just beyond the house, go through the gate and into open fields. The view to the right takes in Tissington and the southern Peak. The lane, now unenclosed, skirts the edge of a long abandoned quarry and still climbing, reaches another gate. To the right, beyond Hollington End Farm, the present main A515 road can be seen, originally a turnpike route built in 1776 to replace Spend Lane.

Beyond the gate, the lane is enclosed again, but is still perched on top of the ridge. Although this road was turnpiked in 1738 it seems certain that it was upgraded from an ancient packhorse route. The route is described in the 1676 edition of Izaak Walton's 'Compleat Angler' where Charles Cotton tells the tale of a journey he made to his home at Beresford Hall near Hartington.

Dewpond

On your left now is a curious ruined barn which seems to be built into the face of an old quarry. Here too are two signposts, one pointing left to Milldale, another with two fingers pointing right. Take the right hand path along the line marked Tissington and head to the right of a clump of trees. There is scant evidence of a path, but the trees are a sure guide as is the dew-pond in the middle of the field. The path crests the ridge and a view of Tissington opens up ahead.

Continue with a wall on your left, the path now descending steeply to a stile in the fence at the bottom of the field. In this next, small field there is a set of railway sleeper gate posts in the bottom left corner. Go through these and across the next narrow field to a step stile by another gateway. Once in the next field go right and diagonally across the field

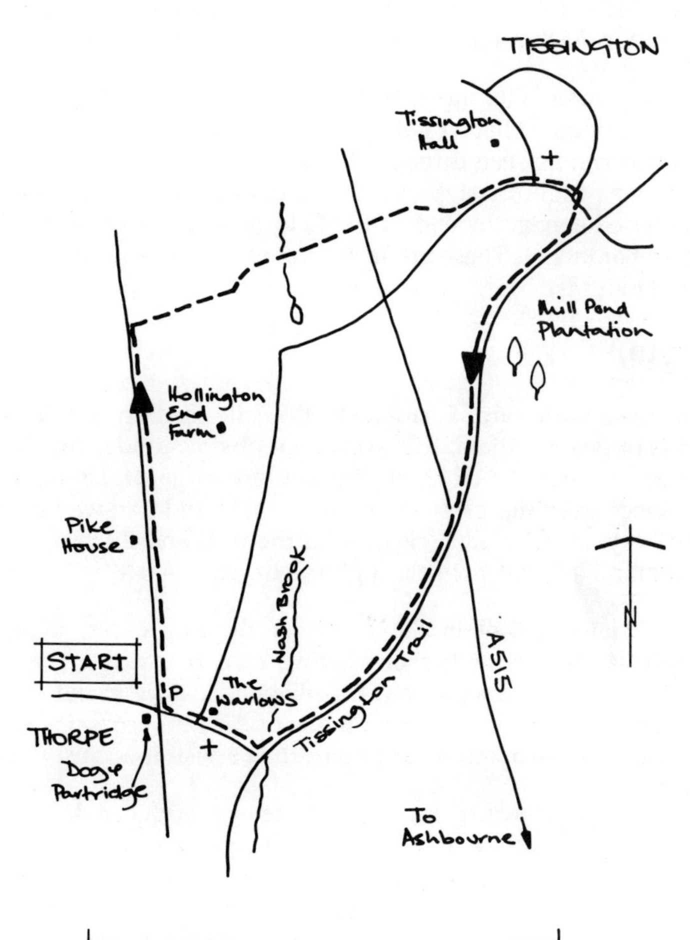
TISSINGTON
Tissington Hall
Mill Pond Plantation
Hollington End Farm
Pike House
START
P
THORPE
The Warlows
Nash Brook
Tissington Trail
Dog & Partridge
A515
To Ashbourne
N
Scale : 1 mile / 1.6km.

which has strong evidence of mediaeval strip field farming shown by the long grassy ridges and the intervening furrows, known as ridge and furrow. In the bottom left hand corner of the field there is a bridge of sorts over a little stream and then a stile into a much larger field which slopes up to the A515 road.

This field also betrays its mediaeval origins with pronounced ridge and furrow in a curious S-shaped pattern. The signpost where the path joins the A515 road can be seen directly ahead so make for this and reach the road by a short flight of steps. Note the construction of the road here, which is carried across the end of the field on a low eighteenth century drystone embankment. These are fairly common in Derbyshire but rarely seen by the motorist.

Tissington

Cross the road with care. Fortunately the stile leading into Tissington parkland is opposite. Again, the path is not obvious under foot but head for the line of trees which mark the western edge of Tissington Hall grounds. Once over the brow of the hill a stile and gateway come into view. The way ahead is then clear, with the wall and ditch on your left and Tissington Hall glimpsed through the trees.

Tissington Estates is still in the hands of the Fitzherbert family who protect this landscape with more loving care than even the strictest conservation area could achieve. The village is a delight and if you are fortunate enough to be in the area on one of the rare occasions when the Hall and gardens are open to the public, then a visit is a must.

Tissington is famous for its well dressings which take place on Ascension Day. In spite of claims from other villages and towns Tissington folk can claim to be the oldest practitioners of the well dressing art. Hall Well is a fine example of a village well. Tissington can get very busy at well dressing time and the easiest way to enter the village is on foot!

Ha Ha

Continue alongside the wall and ditch, a nice example of a Ha Ha, an artificial landscape feature, designed to allow the owner of the mansion to look out of his window over parkland without seeing a wall, but preventing cattle straying into the formal gardens area.

As the path approaches the road, note the avenue of fine limes and then the incongruous red brick houses erected by the London and North Western Railway in the 1890s. Join the road and negotiate a cattle grid to come into the heart of the village. The church is to the left, with its ancient cross in the church yard. The tea shop is on the right, as is the village pond.

Tissington Trail

Go along the road by the pond, passing the site of one of the wells on the left. Then, go right where the sign points to the Tissington Trail Car Park. At the car park go right, along the trail noting the remains of the goods wharf on the right. The trail was once the Buxton to Ashbourne railway line, a belated attempt to get a direct route south out of Buxton. A half hearted attempt was made to capture Buxton to London traffic but it failed miserably. The line was never more than a single track though the bridges were engineered to take two lines.

The former railway now makes for an easy and pleasant walking route. The main A515 road is soon reached again and crossed on a large skew bridge, well known for the number of high sided vehicles trapped beneath it in recent years. Just beyond the bridge was Fenny Bentley goods station. The site of the sidings with the remains of point rodding, gradient post and signal cranks lie hidden in the trees to the left.

Thorpe Cloud

At the next overbridge, you enter the Fenny Bentley cutting nature reserve, then emerge onto a huge embankment over Wash Brook and to Thorpe Cloud station. This is one of those classic British stations, miles away from the place it intended to serve – Dovedale. Go right here and up the station approach, passing the LNWR station house to reach a road just opposite the Narlows car park entrance. The pub is ahead.

WALK 25: WATERHOUSES

The Route: Manifold Trail, Grindon, Deepdale Farm, Back o' th' Brook, Waterfall. There is one climb out of the Manifold but otherwise the going is easy.

Start: Waterhouses Station Car Park. Map ref: 084503

Distance: 9 miles

Map: Ordnance Survey Leisure Map No 24 – The Peak District, White Peak Area

How to get there:

By Bus – The Derby to Manchester (201) bus serves Waterhouses daily. There is a Monday to Saturday local service between Leek and Waterhouses.

By Car – Waterhouses is on the A523 road between Ashbourne and Leek. There is a car park at the old station including cycle hire and toilet block.

The pub featured in this walk is The Red Lion at Waterfall, a friendly house which has served this isolated community well throughout the years. The Landlord, Frank Smith, keeps his beer well serving draught Bass Bitter and Mild from traditional handpumps. The latter drink is unusual for these parts but evidently there are one or two locals with a taste for the brew.

The pub also offers food with a small dining area behind the bar. The rooms are homely, as is the entire pub and while not open on weekday lunchtimes it is open on Saturdays and Sundays. Evening opening varies slightly between Winter and Summer with an earlier start during the light evenings.

The Walk

Start from the car park in Waterhouses, a village in the southernmost stretch of the Peak District lying in Staffordshire. Follow the path out of the car park and cross the lousy A523 before turning left onto the Manifold Trail.

Lea Farm

Follow the track for well over a mile, as far as Lea Farm. You approach a small bridge with Sparrowlee Farm high up on the hillside to your left. Lea Farm is across the river on the right, and serves light refreshments during the summer. Now look for a gate on the left. Go through it and turn right. Walk through another two gates and follow the track as it climbs out of the valley through Little Wood and then passing to the left of a barn.

Walk on to the top left corner of the field, go through a wicket gate and turn right to cross a stile. Proceed ahead through a small paddock to another gate and in the next field head slightly left to a stile by another wicket gate. Once across, head to the left of the barn and to the gate beyond. Follow the line of trees to a further gate leading to a narrow tarmac lane.

For those seeking a short cut, turn left for Waterfall. If your fancy is the longer walk, keep ahead along this lane, through an old white gate with views across to Throwley Moor and Mere Hill. Pass in front of the isolated farmhouse and yard, through the wooden gate ahead and another gate just beyond. Follow the wall on the left down to a gateway and then the old track zig-zags right and left up to another gate. Go through it and keep company with the wall on the left, rising up towards Grindon, soon identified by its conspicuous church spire. Follow the track up to the village, looking out for an old boundary stone marked AH. At the fork turn left and then exit onto a tarmac lane by the Cavalier in Grindon, described in Walk 5, as is the village itself.

If not stopping turn left along the tarmac lane. By Manor Farm take the right fork, passing by old vehicles and as the road climbs gently pass Deepdale Farm and then onto Old fields Farm where you keep ahead by the farm buildings on the right. Just beyond the traditional eighteenth

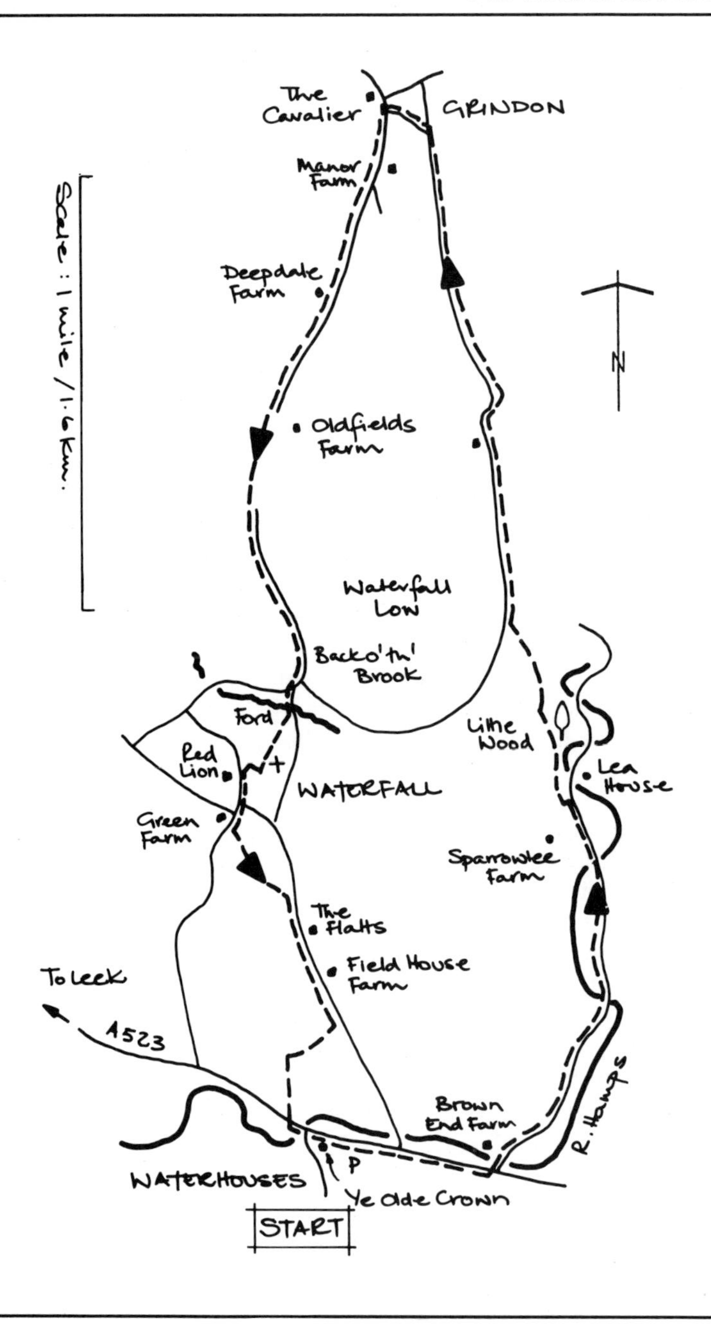
The Cavalier
GRINDON
Manor Farm
Scale : 1 mile / 1.6 km.
Deepdale Farm
N
Oldfields Farm
Waterfall Low
Back o' th' Brook
Ford
Little Wood
Red Lion
WATERFALL
Lea House
Green Farm
Sparrowlee Farm
The Flatts
Field House Farm
To Leek
A523
R. Hamps
Brown End Farm
P
WATERHOUSES
Ye Olde Crown
START

farmhouse the track veers left and right to follow a drystone wall on the right by several small folds. There's a view of quarrying ahead at Cauldon Low, a sharp reminder of our constant demands on the landscape.

Back 'o th' Brook

Go through the gate and follow the lane down to Back o' th' Brook, a quiet little settlement, named no doubt to identify the importance of the brook as a boundary between these dwellings and the remainder of Waterfall. The hamlet has several fascinating buildings.

Turn right and then left to cross the ford, a superb challenge for children, before beginning to climb up the hill. As the lane curves left, stop a moment and look out a gap stile behind the electric telegraph pole on the right. Once through, take a deep breath and climb up the bank with the church coming into sight. Take a glance behind you to Back o' th' Brook and Waterfall Low, thought to be an ancient Bronze Age burial ground.

Waterfall

Look for the gap stile, slightly right, leading into the pleasantly situated churchyard. Waterfall church looks the picture, a simple but romantic place of worship tucked away in the houses of this moorland settlement. The church dates from the twelfth century but was substantially restored in the 1790s. Walk to the gap stile in the top right hand corner of the churchyard. Then head to the left of the Red Lion public house across the field, exiting onto the road by way of two gap stiles next to a stone barn. On the other side of the road stands The Red Lion, a homely pub serving this little community.

Red Lion

Turn right from the entrance to the Red Lion and walk to the junction. To the left is a pocket size village green with stocks and old pump. Turn right, but not right again and not far along go through a gap stile on the left opposite the buildings of Green Farm. Head slightly right across the field through a gap in the next hedge (look for the remains of a stone squeezer stile beneath a tree) and ahead through a small pasture to another stone stile. Keep slightly left to another stone stile and head in the same direction through two more narrow fields with gaps and old stiles in their boundaries. You come to a thick set hedge where a hidden gap stile leads onto a tarmac lane.

Turn right here to pass The Flatts and Field House Farm. Pass a barn on the left and then go right, through a gap stile on your right. Keep company with the wall on the right and, nearing the far wall, cut across left to a makeshift wooden gate. Drop down the narrow strip to cross a stile on the left by a stone hut. Walk through a lush meadow back to a stile by the bridge over the infant Hamps at Waterhouses. Turn left on the main road to return to Ye Olde Crown. Waterhouses car park lies a little way to the right.

Walking in the rain: The Red Lion, appropriately at Waterfall (Courtesy of Chris Rushton, Evening Sentinel)

WALK 26: WENSLEY

The Route: Tearsall, Brightgate, Wynstor rocks, Winster, Ivy House, Clough Wood Lane, Old Millclose, Cambridge Wood

Distance: 5 miles

Start: Wensley Square. Map Reference: 264611

Map: Ordnance Survey Leisure Map No 24 – The Peak District, White Peak Area

How to get there:

By Bus – There is a Monday to Saturday service from Chesterfield, Bakewell and Matlock.

By Car – Travel on the A6 to Darley Dale then on the B5057 to Wensley Square. There is limited parking here.

The Crown is usually open at lunchtimes and at 7 pm in the evenings. The Bowling Green public house in Winster is a large hostelry with lounge, bar and games room offering Mansfield beers and bar meals but it is not always open mid week lunchtimes in Winter. There is a pleasant beer garden at the rear. It is well known amongst walkers and deservedly popular. For those with their own food there is no objection to you eating your sandwiches in the beer garden.

The Walk

The walk starts from Wensley Square, passing the telephone box and the former Crown Inn. Shortly after the old pub, go right, along a lane to leave the village behind. The lane soon becomes a rough track and dips into Wensley Dale. Ahead, on the opposite hillside are a series of terraces, remains of very ancient farming practices. In the dale bottom the track swings left to cross a stream and then rises up the opposite hillside to a gate. At the gate go right, following the tractor ruts up the

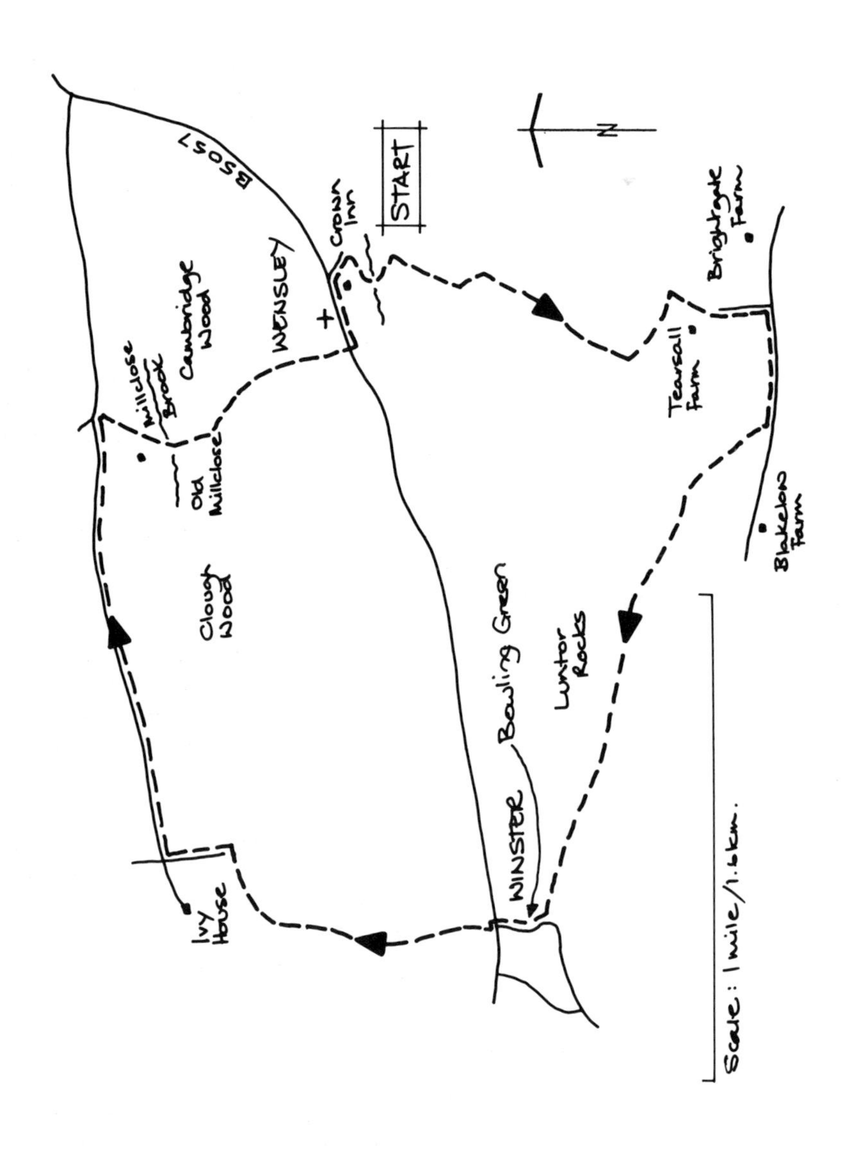
B5057
START
Crown Inn
N
WENSLEY
Cambridge Wood
Millclose Brook
Old Millclose
Clough Wood
Brightgate Farm
Tearsall Farm
Blakelow Farm
Bowling Green
Lunter Rocks
WINSTER
Ivy House
Scale: 1 mile/1.6km.

hill, keeping close to the wall on your left.

There is distinct evidence of early lead mining here and when the end of the field is reached there is quite a deep cut which bars progress in that direction. However, a narrow walled lane goes left and this is followed until it emerges into open fields again. Go right here, heading uphill towards the trees and a spoil heap that marks the site of the old Tearsall mine, now being reworked for fluorspar.

Limestone Fissures

Follow the wall on the right to a stile by a ruined barn. Beyond the barn there is a pond, a conspicuous feature in this limestone area and usually caused by the presence of a bed of clay which prevents the water percolating into the limestone fissures beneath. A prominent track now leads up the hill to a waymark post. The track swings left into Tearsall workings and this was the right of way shown on the map. The blue waymarks, however, offer a diversionary path continuing upwards towards the trees which crown Tearsall Hill. Another waymark post directs you upwards beside the wall.

The limestone in the wall is full of holes like a Gruyere cheese, and there are examples of fossil coral to be found if you look carefully. Some of the limestone has been dolomitised, a process which requires the close proximity of a volcano and not as some locals would have it, the result of the limestone being eaten by a dolomite!

Head now to the left end of the trees where there is a stile, a gate, another blue waymark and an excellent view. Go over a stile and along a track, with Tearsall open cut on your left. The track now swings right and goes through a shallow cutting marking the crest of the hill. Note the rock in the floor and sides of the cutting. Here is the volcanic lava which caused the dolomitisation of the limestone.

Leaving the cutting the track approaches Tearsall Farm and turns left to come up to a road. Ahead, a rough lane continues across Bonsall Moor to Blake Mere and Grange Mill. To the left lies the hamlet of Brightgate. You go right along the road. In a short distance there is a footpath sign on the left. Ignore it. Shortly afterwards, there is one on the right which you follow. Go through the stile into the fields where there is evidence of previous mine workings. Keep to the path. Head for the double pole electricity pylon and find a stile in the corner of the field. The path is not clear but another stile can be seen ahead and the path then occupies a site of a grubbed out wall.

After another stile, the path strikes diagonally across the next two fields, the presence of the stiles being marked by solitary thorn trees. The next field is clipped in the corner, the exit stile being marked by a single large upright stone.

Luntor Rocks

The path now begins its descent towards Winster. Over Haddon, Youlgreave (with its prominent church tower), then Elton village come into sight, followed by the rocks of Robin Hood's Stride. At the corner of the next field there is no stile but a waymarker points left alongside a wall and this is followed until a tree shrouded pile of rocks is reached, a landmark known as Luntor Rocks. The map shows the path as a scramble beneath the rocks but most walkers go right, through a gateway just by the rocks and then turn left to skirt the crags with a wall now on your left.

At the end of the rocks go over a stile. The path crosses the centre of the next field and the line of stiles can be seen in the walls ahead, slanting down to Winster. Eventually, a line of trees is reached and the path threads its way through them. Winster Manor, now an old persons' home, is seen on the right. Head for the green shed and skirt around the back of it.

An obvious path heads diagonally across the field but ignore this and go along the wall at the back of the green shed to a stile in the far wall. A waymark here points down the field, but ignore this too and go over a stile onto a narrow stone terrace. This gets even narrower as it squeezes between houses to emerge on a road by Hope Cottage in Winster. Go right here descending East Bank.

Bowling Green

On the right is the Bowling Green pub. Continue down East Bank to emerge on the main road. To the right is the medieval Market Hall, now a National Trust Information Centre. Winster is a very fine village with some excellent stone buildings on the main street. To the left the Hall is particularly noteworthy. Once the home of a lead mining baron, it is now being restored to its former glories after a period as a pub.

Cross the road and go down the lane by the left side of the GB stores. Passing the playground on the right the lane becomes a rough track and leads through a gate. Just before the track peters out in a rough piece of ground look for a narrow path which bears left through a gap stile. Once in the field, the path is easily followed as it is paved with gritstone blocks which soon lead to a stile in a hawthorn hedge. The paving stones continue again on the other side.

The path descends to a boggy area and the paving stones are lost again. Regain firm ground by the stream. Here the path forks and you go right, crossing another small area of bog, ascending through a gap in a hedge which is presumably where a stile once stood. The stone slabs have gone again but the next stile can be seen ahead, marked with yellow bands. Here, the paving recommences. Crossing another wet patch, the path finally leaves the valley bottom. Go up the field towards the black water tank. Here, go right and cross a small stream to follow the distinct path as it slants quite steeply up the hillside and finally reaches a wooded area.

Mill Close Mine

The path goes over a stile and skirts around a spoil heap, heading to the left to top the rise. Just to the right of Ivy House, it joins a good track, an old packhorse route. Go right here and enjoy an exhilarating mile going steadily downhill. On reaching the wood, it descends steeply. These woods are beautiful in Spring when carpetted with bluebells and other early flowers. The track swings right near a green gate, a rear entrance to a works and then forks. Go right here to a black gate.

Once past the gate the track forks again. Go right here to the impressive remains of old Mill Close engine house. This was built for a Newcomen engine in 1748 to drain the mine. The engine operated until 1764 when production ceased. When the shaft was re-opened in 1859 a new engine was installed, continuing to work until 1874.

Make your way down to the track you left at the black gate and now go down to the valley bottom. There is a gateway ahead just beyond the stream. Cross the stream on the culvert (the footbridge is unsafe), then go right through the gateway, towards a fence to pick up a narrow path heading up the hillside. Ignore paths and tracks going straight up from the gate.

Cambridge Wood

As the path reaches the wood it broadens and becomes a pronounced track. This is Cambridge Wood, scene of a celebrated dispute over quarter cord. This was an ancient lead mining custom whereby the miner was entitled to a quarter of a meer (a meer being between 27 and 32 yards) either side of the vein of ore, on which to deposit his spoil, build his hut and so on. The vein on this hillside was so wide and complex that the landowners argued that to lose a further 6 to 8 yards either side of the vein was excessive and hence the bitter argument.

The track continues steeply uphill, passing a pond nearly at the top, finally emerging from the wood at a stile. The path continues with the fence to the left, passing a covered reservoir then another pond before swinging to the right to avoid a farm yard just prior to reaching a road.

Cross the road onto the footway and go left, passing the Red Lion Inn on the left and continuing along by the Reading Room to The Square in Wensley.

WALK 27: WETTON

The Route: From hill to vale by Thor's cave and alongside the Manifold which is for the best part of the year dry. Return by Beeston Tor. There are one or two strenuous climbs on the route.

Distance: 4 to 5 miles

Start: Royal Oak public house, Wetton. Map Reference: 109554

Map: Ordnance Survey Outdoor Leisure Map No 24 – The Peak District, White Peak Area.

How to get there:

By Bus – Very limited service from Ashbourne, Buxton and Leek on weekdays and Summer Sundays

By Car – Follow instructions as for Alstonefield, then as signed via Hope. There is limited parking near to the public toilets in the village.

Ye Olde Royal Oak, more commonly known as The Royal Oak, is a friendly pub, thought to date from the seventeenth century or earlier with plenty of room for the walker. It offers bar food and draught ales including Theakston's Best Bitter and Ruddles County on handpull. There are several cosy nooks about the bar and a piano surrounded by sheet music and mementoes of the player's previous career.

The Royal Oak is usually open during lunchtimes and evenings throughout the week. It provides a respite for those who seek the middle ground between the Manifold and Dove. The villagers tend to be outnumbered but this is now true of many a Peak District pub which stay in business by catering for the passing trade.

Wetton is a charming village, at one time an agricultural centre and now reliant more on tourism. The inn and church stand in the centre of the community side by side. The middle of the village is designated a conservation area.

The Walk

From the Royal Oak turn left and at the corner left again through the village and past the church on your left. A junction is reached and shortly after a track branches left. Walk on the road a few paces more to cross a stile on the left into a field. Walk down the middle of this field to cross another very narrow gap stile. The views are exquisite with the spire of Grindon church being a dominant landmark here as on other walks in the book.

Continue mid way down the dry valley with the path leading into woodland and scrub. Do not take any of the left turnings unless you

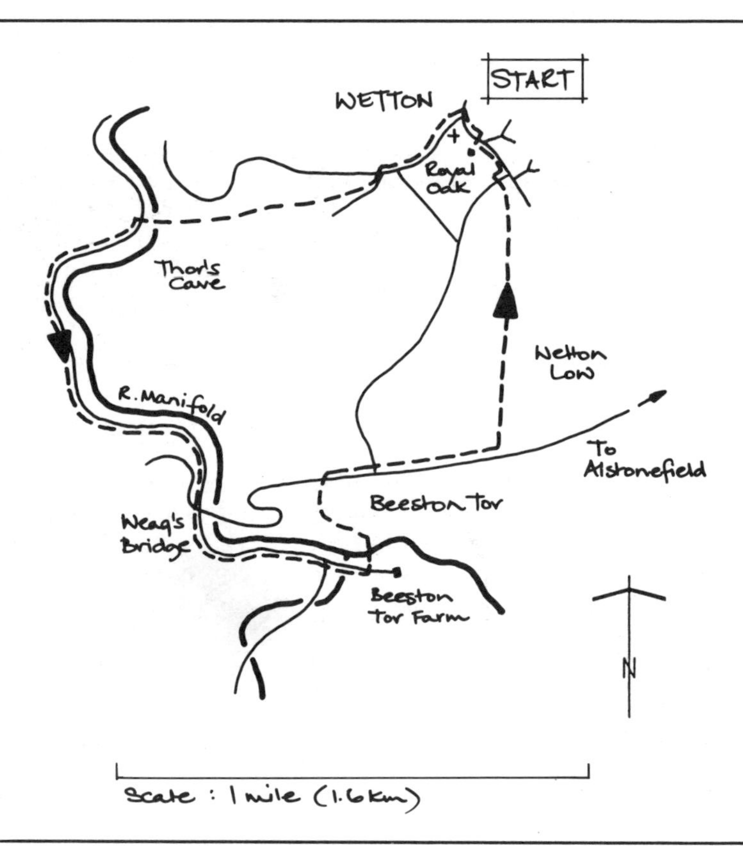

wish to divert to Thor's Cave, with its huge entrance. This cave almost certainly was the home of prehistoric humankind.

Otherwise follow the well trodden path down to the footbridge and over to the Manifold trail, a former railway line now populated by cyclists and walkers.

Turn left and walk along the trail for a mile to Weag's Bridge where it is crossed by a tarmac lane. Be warned. If there has been heavy rain and the water runs deep in the river bed, turn left here and walk up the winding tarmac lane. If there is no river or a trickle keep ahead.

Beeston Tor

Beyond here there is a parallel road to the trail. Follow it around a curve and then along the straight section. Cross a stile on the left onto the access road to Beeston Tor Farm passing the old refreshment room at

The Old Refreshment Room, Beeston Tor

one time serving Beeston Tor station. This was operated by a Mr Wood who was one of a very few people who travelled on the first and last train to use the line. There were only seven passengers on the last train.

Once across the bridge and through the gate look for a path down to the riverside and stepping stones. This is easy when there is no or little water but rather difficult after heavy rain. On the other side the path curves right and then left around a perimeter fence. Then climb up the steep edge of Beeston Tor following the path which curves right, between scrub and scree, and finally to give out into a field. Keep ahead for the last section up to the tarmac lane coming up from Weag's Bridge.

Turn right but not before pausing for an exceptional view over the Staffordshire Moorlands. The road climbs out of the valley to a summit where you go through a gateway on the left near to an old lime kiln full of dumped material. Head to the right of the stone barn to cross a squeezer stile and then continue in the same direction to a gateway. Once over, bear left to a stone stile over a wall. Wetton can now be seen over the fields.

The path leads slightly right across this field, to the left of a tree near you, to a stone stile just to the left of another tree at the opposite side of the field. The path heads in a similar direction through a series of narrow fields by way of stiles before entering a final field. Here it curves left to a gate which gives out onto a tarmac lane. Go right and at the junction left into Wetton.

WALK 28: WINSTER

The Route: Bank Top, Islington Lane, Elton Cross, Dudwood Lane, Birchover, Ivy House, Winster. A pleasant real ale ramble with one or two climbs.

Distance: 3 miles

Start: The Miners Standard, Winster Bank Top. Map Reference: 238603

Map: Ordnance Survey Outdoor Leisure Map No 24 – The Peak District, White Peak Area.

How to get there:

By Bus – There is a Monday to Saturday service from Matlock, Bakewell and Chesterfield to the centre of Winster which is ten minutes walk to Bank Top. Alight at the Market Hall and walk up East Bank to its junction with West Bank to Bank Top.

By Car – Travel to Winster Bank Top on the B5057 from Darley Dale or the B5056 from the A6 at Piccory Corner or from the A5012 from Grangemill.

There is limited car parking on West Bank off the main road.

Winster Bank Top is a separate little hamlet clustered around the cross roads formed by the B5056 and the minor road known as West Bank and Elton Common Road. There are a couple of farms, a pleasantly restored 'ore' house, a recently dredged and revitalised mere and a pub, The Miners Standard. For those who relate the word 'standard' to flags it is surprising to see the inn sign depicting a dish. The ore dish was the standard measure given to the lead miners by the monarch, hence the name. The dish would have been checked by the senior official of the leadminers court, the Barmote, and every lead miner had to prove that his mine was capable of supplying a dish of good ore before being allowed to continue working. The standard dish is still kept at the Barmote Court in Wirksworth.

The Miners Standard pub is also well known to ramblers for the Saville's are keen walkers themselves, not only in the UK but also in central Europe. They welcome ramblers at this multi-roomed pub, replete with miners memorabilia. On offer is a superb pint of Marstons Pedigree or Theakstons XB and a guest beer. Jane, Lynda and Brian Saville also serve food both at lunchtime and early evening. Pub opening hours are from noon until 3pm (2.30 pm in Winter) and from 7pm in the evening, although in the height of summer they open at 6pm on Mondays to Fridays.

For those who enjoy camping there is a site behind the pub for canvas lovers. The Miners Standard is not a pub to be missed.

The Walk

Leaving The Miners Standard turn right to the crossroads at the top of the hill. On the left is the Mere and on the right the restored orehouse. A little further along the main road near Bonsall Moor junction is a stone guide stoop on the right now serving as a gate post. One of the signs indicates 'Leek' but of this road there is no trace.

At the crossroads, go right and at the next crossroads turn right again onto a narrow rough lane. This is Islington Lane, at one time an important route. This soon becomes a fine green lane sunken between limestone walls. There are views across to Wardlow Hay Cop, Robin Hood's Stride and Stanton Moor.

Elton Cross

The lane descends to a junction but keep straight on, climbing gently before descending again to another cross roads. This is Elton Cross and a public house once stood on the opposite corner. It ceased to exist when the 'new' road was built in the nineteenth century and has been excavated recently. Alas, the cellars were found to be empty!

Ignoring the tarmac road to the right and left, follow the narrow lane downwards. This is Dudwood Lane, part of the Old Portway. The lane descends quite steeply until Dudwood Farm is reached. Just past this, go

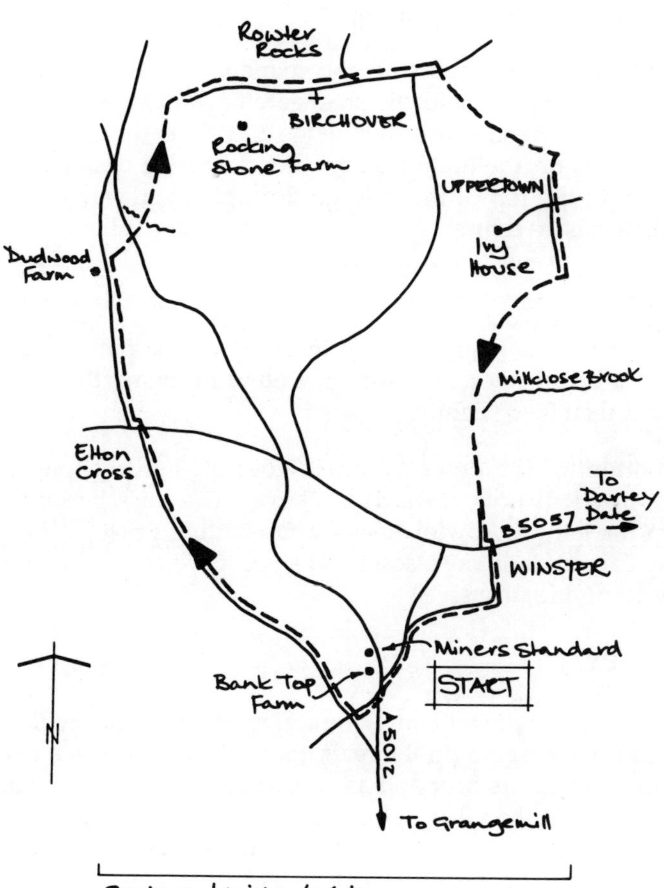
Rowter Rocks
BIRCHOVER
Rocking Stone Farm
UPPERTOWN
Ivy House
Dudwood Farm
Millclose Brook
Elton Cross
To Darley Dale
B5057
WINSTER
Miners Standard
Bank Top Farm
START
A5012
N
To Grangemill
Scale: 1 mile/1.6 km.

through a stile on the right and cross the field diagonally towards the camping sign to another stile. This gives out into the main road. Take care here as there is neither verge or footway. Cross the road to another stile to the right of the camping sign and on the left hand side of the driveway. This leads into fields again.

Descend to the stream passing the manhole cover as a marker. The crossing can be muddy and the stile/gate beyond is of unusual design! Keep to the right hand side of the hedge and climb the slope towards the clump of pines on the hilltop. Robin Hood's Stride dominates the view on the left. At the top of the field go through a gateway and come to a lane which has a central spine of paving slabs. When the pines are reached there is a junction of paths.

Your path is joined by one coming from Uppertwon (right) and another coming up from the main road. Continue along the path ahead which is now quite a broad track as it swings around to the north of the Rocking Stones and then falls slightly.

At the bottom of the descent a track goes off left but ignore this and carry on, upwards now, towards Birchover. The track becomes a tarmac road. On the left are Rowtor Rocks, a fascinating gritstone outcrop with curiously carved doorways, seats and steps, caves and scrambles as well as many terrifying drops!

Birchover

The lane passes Birchover church on the right and then the Druid Inn on the left before emerging on the main road. The Druid has a considerable reputation both for its beer and as an eating house. At the main road go straight ahead up the village street, passing the Red Lion Inn on the left, a fine public house serving a range of draught beers and light snacks. Inside the front door is a well, which has a thick glass cover over it. It is quite a fright when the lights in the well are switched on and you're standing on the glass.

Leaving the Red Lion go left and pass the lane leading to Uppertown and Winster and a short distance further on, seek out the path on the right which leads through a series of fields before turning sharp right to emerge on the cart road near Ivy House. Go straight on at this point, through the gateway to come to spoil heaps of an erstwhile lead mine. The path skirts the heaps on the left to reach a stile at the head of a steep drop down to Millclose Brook. The path now bears right passing a large conical shaped depression which is probably a run in shaft (so do not go near) and then slants steeply down the hillside to a crossing of a stream. Go left here by a black plastic water tank and cross the field which according to the ordnance survey map is a wood.

Winster is in view on the opposite hillside but there are a few trials yet to come! The path dips down a muddy bank to cross a streamlet, beyond which there is a stile in a hedge and a section of paved path. Continue ahead with Winster in your sights to reach a gap in the hedge opposite.

Beyond this the path slips into a wet area with a vague path. The right of way strikes across the bog and straight up the hillside to a stile in the thick thorn hedge ahead. Some locals skirt the boggy area to the left hand end of the hedge and then go right to regain the proper route. The path beyond the wet area is marked with paving slabs. Once through the hedge the stone slabs reappear. Continue across the field to a stile so meeting a narrow lane which leads unerringly into Winster Main Street, which is a particularly fine example of eighteenth and nineteenth century buildings.

Mining Boom

At one time, at the height of the lead mining boom, Winster reputedly had more pubs than Chesterfield. Now, however, the lead industry has gone and the village has recently been discovered by commuters. The Market Hall, now owned by The National Trust, is well worth as visit. Nearby is Winster Hall, a fine mansion built for a lead baron.

Go up East Bank, passing the Bowling Green pub on the left, which features in the Wensley walk. Continue to climb up East Bank to join another lane, West Bank and thereby reach The Miners Standard.

WALK 29: WIRKSWORTH

The Route: Wirksworth, Breamfield, Broadgate, Alport Heights, Hole-house, Gorsey Bank

Distance: 3 miles

Start: Wirksworth Market Place. Map Reference: 287540

Map: Ordnance Survey Outdoor Leisure Map No 24 – The Peak District, White Peak Area.

How to get there:

By Bus – There are daily buses from Bakewell, Derby and Matlock.

By Car – Travel on the B5023 from Derby and Matlock. There is Pay and Display parking in the marketplace or on street parking elsewhere.

There are several public houses in Wirksworth to choose from but one favourite of the authors, in the marketplace, is the Blacks Head. The pub is instantly recognisable by the cheerful, grinning, turbanned head on its sign. An old inn, the beamed roof in the bar said to date from the 1700s, and with open fires, it has a pleasant atmosphere. The beers are Kimberley ales, cask conditioned Best Bitter and Classic on handpulls. Food is served at lunchtime.

Wirksworth is an ancient market town, at least of Saxon origin and most probably earlier. The town itself is situated on limestone rock but to the east rise the shale and gritstone hills of Black Rocks, Bole Hill and Alport Heights. The name Bole Hill provides a clue to the town's earlier economic base, which was the production of lead. The lead ore (Galena) was extracted from the numerous lead veins in the limestone and was smelted in primitive furnaces, known as boles, on nearby gritstone hills.

Wirksworth is still heavily influenced by the minerals industry, with a number of limestone quarries and fluorspar workings nearby. The town is to this day the headquarters of the lead mining court, The Barmote, which adjudicates on mineral disputes. Wirksworth is full of fine buildings, has a superb heritage centre and is home to the National Stone Centre so it makes for a good day outing.

The Walk

Start from the marketplace by going over the pedestrian crossing then almost immediately left into a narrow alleyway which leads between buildings and soon emerges in the church yard. This is more like a cathedral close than a parish church yard as there are so many splendid buildings surrounding it. The almhouses and old grammar school, now a woodworking building are splendid. If only the church spire was more dramatic. A church of such quality deserves better. The church is dedicated to St Mary. It has some particularly fine Saxon carvings depicting the Last Supper, the life of Christ and also of lead mining, so you might choose to take a look inside at the fine interior.

Leave the close by the path to the right of the almshouses and follow this down past the playing fields to the railway line. Turn right here.

The Wirksworth branch line has had a chequered history, first being envisaged as part of a main line from Derby to Manchester, then relegated to a branch, losing its passenger service on the cold morning of January 1st, 1949. Since then it has remained open for mineral traffic but there is none at present although it is still 'officially' open (November 1993) despite half a mile of track being lifted at a strategic point.

Continue alongside the railway line until the end of the first set of playing fields. At this point there is a path off to the left to a stone bridge across the infant Ecclesbourne. Once over the bridge, go right alongside the stream to the remains of a stile, then left up the steps to cross the railway line.

On the other side of the line, negotiate another stile and bear right along a distinct path heading diagonally across a field to a gap in the hedge. Once reached, follow a track onwards and upwards towards the clump of Scots pine. There is a stile and gateway to the right of the pines. Beyond this stile there are two gateways on the left. Go left, through the stile by a second gateway and join a track coming up from Gorseybank, the houses of which can be seen to the right.

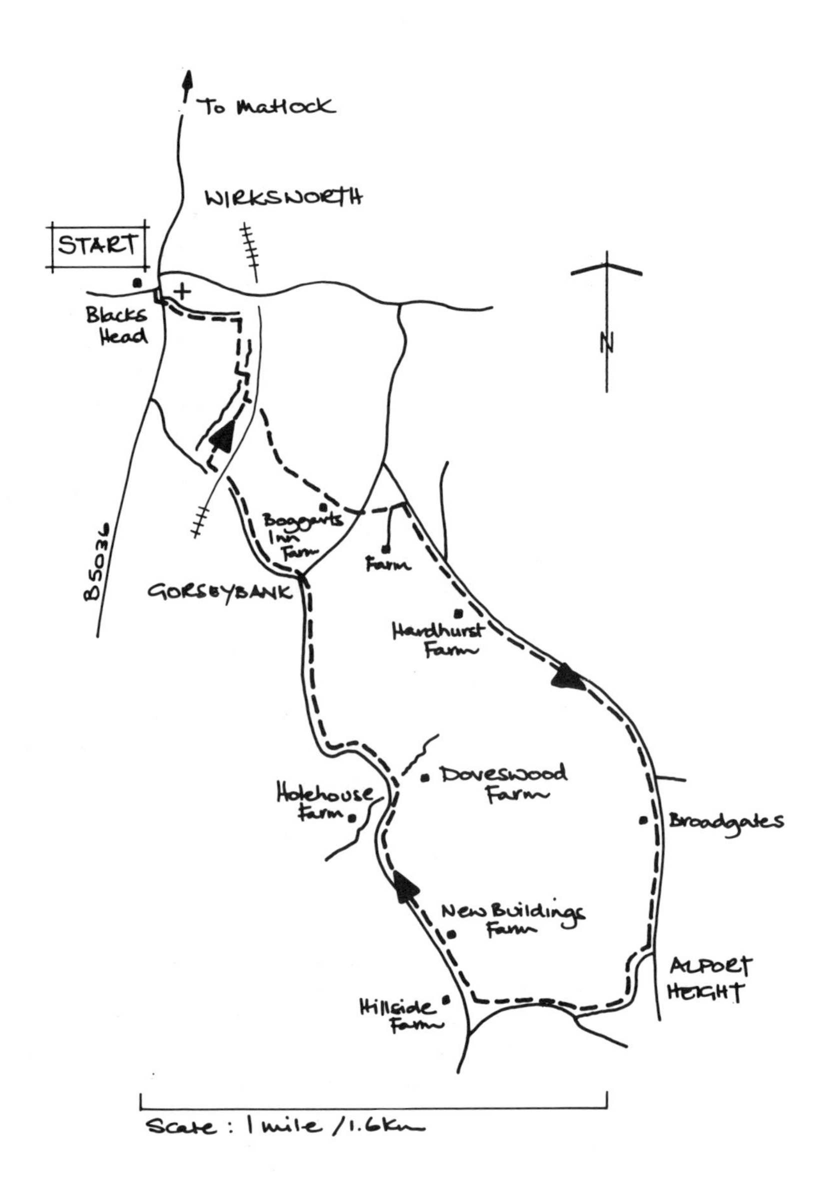
To Matlock
WIRKSWORTH
START
Blacks Head
N
Boggarts Inn Farm
Farm
B5036
GORSEYBANK
Hardhurst Farm
Doveswood Farm
Holehouse Farm
Broadgates
New Buildings Farm
ALPORT HEIGHT
Hillside Farm
Scale : 1 mile / 1.6km

Boggart Inn Farm

The track now goes steadily up the hill, but where it turns right to the delightfully named Boggart Inn Farm, keep straight on by a hedge, heading for a stile to the left of a little blue hut.

From this stile there is a good view back over Wirksworth to Middleton Top. Continue up the hill by a hedge, but almost at the top of the field there is a stile in the new fence on the left. This is the line of the path, though most people seem to carry on a few yards further up the field and go through the gate. Follow the path over the stile to another just to the right of and half hidden by a hedge. The route disgorges into a narrow rough lane, where you go left and then almost immediatley right through a stile, to head steeply uphill, keeping well to the left of the farm.

The farm access track is crossed and another squeeze stile leads into a further steep sloped field. The exit can be seen ahead, a gap stile leading into a lane.

Old Portway

Emerging on the lane, go right and follow the lane up to the junction near Hardhurst Farm. There are fine views to the right over the Ecclesbourne valley and back to Wirksworth with the white of the limestone standing out quite starkly. This lane was probably part of the old Portway, from which Alport takes its name. Nothing to do with the sea here, it is derived from 'portage' or carrying.

Continue along the lane, which sees very few cars, keeping slightly right or straight on at each junction until a crossroads is reached after about a mile. This spot is known as Alport Height, a former beacon site and now used by the police for radio communications. Carry on ahead for a short way, then leave the road to climb up past the huge standing stone and a stone guide post. The latter was built in about 1709 and points the way to Derby. At that time this was the main road from Wirksworth to Derby. The big standing stone probably served as a marker tor. It can be seen prominently from the Portway, miles to the south.

The view from the top of the Heights is very extensive ranging from the Trent Power stations to Charnwood Forest in the south, through to

Harboro Rocks and the White Peak in the north and west. Retrace your steps back to the crossroads and go left to commence the descent to Wirksworth. The lane drops steeply with views of the Ecclesbourne valley. This name is thought to derive from the Latin *ecclesia* which is the root for the Welsh *eglwys* and the French *église*. Its occurrence in England as the place name Eccles normally indicates a Christian church or community persisting through the late Roman period and Dark Ages into early Saxon times.

Doveswood Brook

Keep right at the next road junction and continue to descend until the road swings left. At this point a path continues straight on, dropping steeply across the field to emerge on another lane near Hillside Farm. Go right here along the narrow lane, passing Hillside Farm on the left and New Buildings Farm on the right. The lane begins to descend more steeply into into the valley of Doveswood Brook and passes Holehouse Farm on the left. Keep on the lane which now deteriorates to a rough track as it approaches a stream. The track swings left to cross the stream by a little bridge near to Doveswood farm. Beyond the bridge it rises away from the brook and a choice of route becomes available.

The track continues as a deep cut hollow way, a sure sign of antiquity and previous heavy use. It is now a haven for wildlife. To say that it can be wet is an understatement, so if it has been raining the alternative route might be preferable. Use the field path on the right, closely paralleling the hollow way. The path is not distinct but the stiles are all in place and the hollow way is an unerring guide. After nearly half a mile, the path rejoins the hollow way via a stile on the left. Immediatley on the left hand side of the hollow way is another stile and the path recommences on the other side, i.e. with the hollow way now to your right. After a field the path rejoins the track again and then gives out onto a tarmac lane leading down through the older part of Gorseybank.

Follow the road down through the more modern housing and then left down to the railway level crossing. Turn right just after the crossing and follow the path alongside the railway line to the point where you crossed the line on the outward journey. Retrace your steps back to Wirksworth marketplace for a well-earned rest.

WALK 30: YOULGREAVE

The Route: Bradford, Rounds Wood, Harthill Moor, Hopping Farm, Bradford Dale

Distance: 3 to 4 miles

Start: George Hotel. Map Reference: 212644

Map: Ordnance Survey Outdoor Leisure Map No 24 – The Peak District, White Peak Area.

How to get there:

By Bus – There are buses on Mondays to Saturdays from Matlock, Bakewell and Chesterfield.

By Car – Travel on the A6 to Piccory Corner then on the B5056 to Hawley's Bridge. Use the unclassified road to Youlgreave. There is limited on street parking in the village. Please park considerately.

The George Hotel is a homely sort of pub with handpulled Home Mild and Bitter. The landlord, John Brindley, welcomes walkers in the tap room without removing boots and if you wish, you can eat your own sandwiches in this room. Most people, however, partake of the bar food available.

Prince Charles once called at the pub with Princess Alexandra for a toilet break and the landlord's late father had a photo taken with the Prince. The picture now proudly hangs in the front bar with a little ditty concocted by friends. For those who enjoy sitting outside there are a few picnic tables, but the joy of this pub is the atmosphere indoors, not to mention the well-kept beers.

Youlgreave is renowned for its well dressing ceremonies. It also has its own water company, and a stone tank dating from 1829 can still be seen in the main street. There is an annual village pantomime and an active youth hostel. The church, which dominates the main street, is visible for miles around and is well worth browsing around.

The Walk

Leaving the George, go down a lane opposite with the church to your left and the Green Apple on the right. The road descends to Bradford, a name which presumably derives from 'Broadford'. The road crosses the river on a culvert. To the right is the path through Bradford Dale, along which you will return. There used to be a small garage on the far bank of the river which could only be approached by driving the car into the water!

Mawstone Mine

As the lane climbs towards the council houses, there is a stile on the left and the footpath leads off across fields. Ahead can be seen the grassed over tops of Mawstone mine, a lead mine closed in 1932 following a gas explosion which killed eight workers. Although common in coal mining, gas explosions were mercifully rare in lead mining, as the workings were carried out mainly in limestone rocks. However, the mines between Bradford Dale and the Derwent at Darley Dale were worked through shales and gritstones and were prone to 'firedamp'. Also seen from this point is Castle Ring, an Iron Age hill fort crowning a flat topped hill.

The path slants diagonally across the field to another stile, then runs alongside a wall to a further stile. Cross the next small field with a small lake to the left. After the next field is crossed the path enters a larger enclosure from which there is no obvious exit, as it is hidden by the slope of the land. Head towards Castle Ring and a stile soon comes into view when crossing the marshy area surrounding Bleakley Dike, a place to muddy your boots.

The path begins to climb quite steeply and becomes a wide dark green track. It passes another stile in a derelict hedge with many gaps and then slants left across the next field to yet another stile and so gains an obvious tractor route which goes left around the hillside. This is shown as Roundwood on the map but the wood has now gone.

The track swings around the hillside into a short valley with Castle Ring rising steeply on the left. At the point where the track rejoins the valley floor a path goes off left up the slopes of the fort but this is not followed.

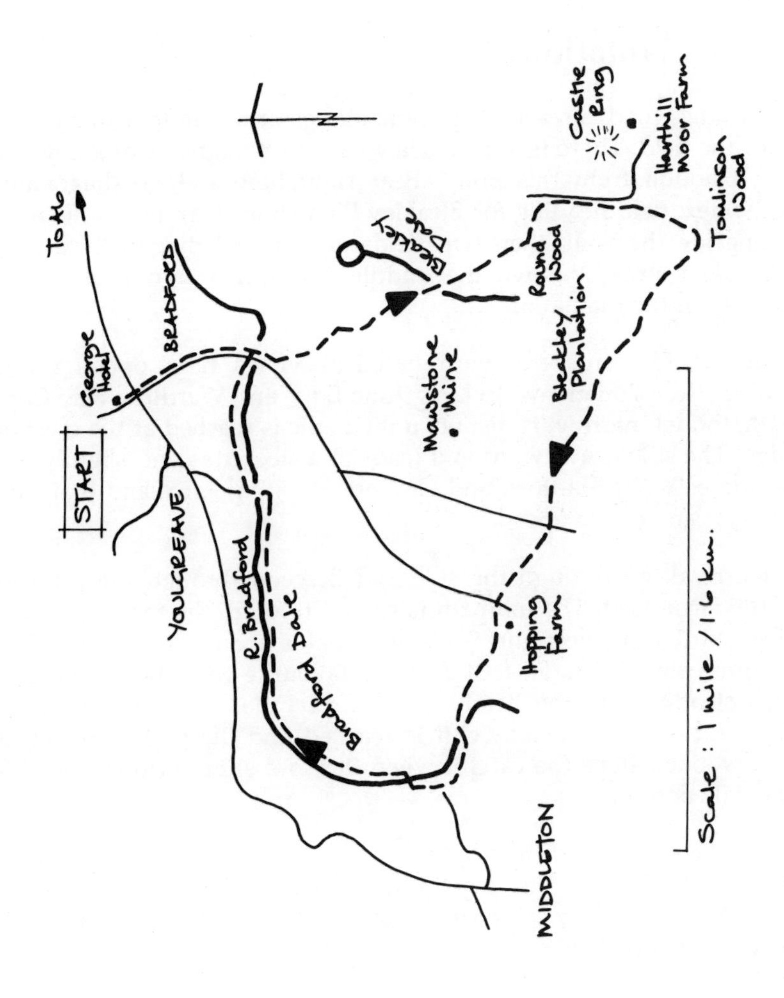
To A6
START
George Hotel
BRADFORD
YOULGREAVE
R. Bradford
Bradford Dale
MIDDLETON
Mawstone Mine
Hopping Farm
Bleakley Plantation
Bleakley Dale
Round Wood
Tomlinson Wood
Harthill Moor Farm
Castle Ring
N
Scale : 1 mile / 1.6 km.

Carry on up the track instead, to a gate where a main track goes left to Harthill Moor Farm and a path carries straight on here in a south west direction heading for the right hand end of Tomlinson's Wood. The route is signed.

Bleakley Plantation

Just before the wood is reached, go right alongside a wall to a stile in the corner of the field. There is a good view back to Youlgreave and beyond to Over Haddon from this point. Bear right here and go diagonally across the next field heading for Bleakley Plantation. Turn left at the next stile alongside the wall, then two fields are crossed diagonally and a third is taken straight down the middle to reach a sign post at the southern tip of the plantation.

Continue straight on here, with excellent views now opening out northwards over Youlgreave to Longstone Edge and Wardlow Hay Cop. The path, though narrow, is distinct until a stile is reached at the crest of the ridge. The stile is awkward and leads to a steep descent, slightly left to the lane between Bradford and Gratton. Hopping Farm and its fields of caravans can be seen ahead.

Cross the road, go through the stile and descend through the caravan site to the farm itself. The footpath is signed through the farm complex, which is skirted on the right. Soon open fields are reached again. The path is quite obvious under foot as it is a favourite with the caravaners. It drops steadily into the head of Bradford Dale. The entry is quite dramatic, for a low limestone cliff is reached and the path descends a flight of wooden steps (be careful when they are slippy) down the cliff into the dale bottom.

Go across the stream and then right down the valley, ignoring the paths going left to Middleton. The path skirts a small mill pond then swings right to cross the dam by some ruined buildings to pick up a broad track on the far side of the river.

Sparkling Waters

There follows a delightful mile down one of Derbyshire's most beautiful dales alongside sparkling waters flowing into fish pools watched equally eagerly by birds and fishermen. Look out for the dabchicks, herons, kingfishers and a variety of ducks, moorhen and coot.

At the stone slab bridge, go left and cross the river to reach the foot of Holy Well. This lane gives a quick ascent to the centre of Youlgreave if needed but otherwise go right and continue along the north side of the river through pleasant meadows back to Bradford. From this point retrace your steps back up to The George.

The Village Pump, Alstonefield

MORE PUB WALKS!

Sample the delights of even more country pubs, and enjoy some of the finest walks with our expanding range of real ale books:

PUB WALKS IN THE PEAK DISTRICT – Les Lumsdon and Martin Smith

MORE PUB WALKS IN THE PEAK DISTRICT – Les Lumsdon and Martin Smith

PUB WALKS IN LANCASHIRE – Neil Coates

PUB WALKS IN THE PENNINES – Les Lumsdon and Colin Speakman

PUB WALKS IN THE LAKE DISTRICT – Neil Coates

PUB WALKS IN THE YORKSHIRE DALES – Clive Price

HEREFORDSHIRE WALKS – REAL ALE AND CIDER COUNTRY – Les Lumsdon

PUB WALKS IN CHESHIRE – Jen Darling

And there are even more books for outdoor people in our catalogue, including:

EAST CHESHIRE WALKS – Graham Beech

WEST CHESHIRE WALKS – Jen Darling

WEST PENNINE WALKS – Mike Cresswell

NEWARK AND SHERWOOD RAMBLES – Malcolm McKenzie

RAMBLES AROUND MANCHESTER – Mike Cresswell

WESTERN LAKELAND RAMBLES – Gordon Brown

WELSH WALKS: Dolgellau and the Cambrian Coast – Laurence Main

OFF-BEAT CYCLING IN THE PEAK DISTRICT – Clive Smith

THE GREATER MANCHESTER BOUNDARY WALK – Graham Phythian

And there's more . . .

We also publish:

Guidebooks for local towns

Spooky stories

Football books

and, under our Sigma Press banner,
over 100 computer books!

All of our books are available from your local bookshop.

In case of difficulty, or to obtain our complete catalogue, please contact:

Sigma Leisure,
1 South Oak Lane,
Wilmslow, Cheshire SK9 6AR

Phone: 0625 - 531035 Fax: 0625 - 536800

ACCESS and VISA orders welcome!